Henry Tipper

The Growth and Influence of Music in Relation to Civilization

Henry Tipper

The Growth and Influence of Music in Relation to Civilization

ISBN/EAN: 9783337086992

Printed in Europe, USA, Canada, Australia, Japan

Cover: Foto ©Thomas Meinert / pixelio.de

More available books at **www.hansebooks.com**

THE
GROWTH AND INFLUENCE OF MUSIC IN RELATION TO CIVILIZATION.

To

MY MOTHER AND SISTERS.

The Growth and Influence of Music in Relation to Civilization.

BY

H. TIPPER.

'Here will we sit, and let the sounds of music
Creep in our ears.'
'MERCHANT OF VENICE.'

LONDON:
ELLIOT STOCK, 62, PATERNOSTER ROW, E.C.
1898.

PREFACE.

THE purpose of this volume is to consider the growth and development of music chiefly in relation to the moral influence it has exerted, and the ideal forces of which it is the exponent. To this end an earnest study has been given to the subject from the aspects indicated, and an attempt made to show how in each period, school and composer is reflected the peculiar characteristics of the time which may be under consideration. The four chapters on China, Hindustan, Egypt, and Israel are, however, not designed as an examination of Eastern music. Introduced to give unity to the subject, the national idiosyncrasies which found expression in their art have been but briefly dwelt upon, but as the work progresses, the idea upon which it is based assumes increasing prominence, especially in the essays upon the great composers, Bach, Handel, Gluck, Haydn, Mozart, and Beethoven. That such a design is worthily fulfilled is too much to hope. Still, to the lover of art in general, and to the lover of music in particular, a perusal of the work may leave an impression of the majesty and permanence of ideal forces, which the tendency of the time has unwittingly done much to obscure.

It will doubtless be remarked that the art as developed in England has not received consideration. This is so, because it was desired to reserve the subject for separate treatment, and also that the narrative of the main development of music in Western Europe, as apart from England, should not be interrupted. Further, the volume ends with the death of Beethoven, but if the method of study here indicated should prove interesting, it can easily be pursued upon similar lines. Finally, among many authorities upon general musical history, especial mention must be made of the History of Music by Emil Naumann, the interesting volumes in the 'Great Musician' Series, and last, though not least, Sir George Grove's 'Dictionary of Musicians.'

H. TIPPER.

IVER, LOWER ROAD,
   SUTTON,
      SURREY.

CONTENTS.

THE BIRTH OF THE ART IN THE EAST AND THE WEST.

		PAGE
I.	INTRODUCTION	1
II.	CHINA	3
III.	HINDUSTAN	7
IV.	EGYPT	10
V.	ISRAEL	15
VI.	GREECE	20

THE EARLY CHRISTIAN AND MIDDLE AGES.

VII.	THE ADVENT OF THE SPIRIT OF LOVE	37
VIII.	MUSIC AND THE EARLY CHURCH	43
IX.	THE TROUBADOURS AND MINNESINGERS	48
X.	THE EARLIEST FRENCH SCHOOL	52
XI.	THE GALLO-BELGIC SCHOOL	56
XII.	THE NETHERLAND SCHOOL	59

THE PERIOD OF THE RENAISSANCE.

XIII.	THE RENAISSANCE	65
XIV.	THE INFLUENCE OF LUTHER	68
XV.	VENICE AND ADRIAN WILLAERT	72

		PAGE
XVI.	ROME AND PALESTRINA	76
XVII.	ROME AND ORATORIO	80
XVIII.	OPERA	84
XIX.	LOTTI AND FRESCOBALDI	92
XX.	NAPLES AND SCARLATTI	94
XXI.	FRENCH OPERA	99
XXII.	THE PRECURSORS OF THE GREAT TONE POETS	105

THE GREAT TONE POETS.

XXIII.	JOHANN SEBASTIAN BACH	117
XXIV.	HANDEL	138
XXV.	GLUCK	159
XXVI.	HAYDN	171
XXVII.	MOZART	188
XXVIII.	BEETHOVEN	200
	INDEX	217

THE BIRTH OF THE ART IN THE EAST AND THE WEST.

I.

INTRODUCTION.

AT certain periods in the history of civilization there have been vouchsafed to man visions of ideal beauty which, according to the age and circumstance, he has endeavoured substantially to realize now in one form of art and now in another. Of these arts there is one, that of tone, whereby the abstract is made real and the ideal is attained. Tone—Music—summons Nature's laws and they obey, and by her inspiration man, not infrequently, finds his solace in repentance, and his utterance perfected in the chorale of the universe.

Many, as we regard them, of the great primal movements of mankind were from East to West, from the rising to the setting sun. Through the pale morning light of human thought and history, and the shadowy mists of a poetic mythology, comes sounding from the East the voice of music. From the heart of Nature it passed into the heart of man; from the heart of man it reascends to God, from whence it came. Man's soul is but a lyre through which the emotions sweep, and every breath of universe and every changeful tone vibrates within him through consciousness and sympathy. We claim for art that it is a manifestation of the Divine Soul; we recognise it as a Father's gift to His children whereby to glorify the material, and to open upon the mind the vista of immortal beauty.

Throughout Nature we see the working of the progressive principle, and if there is one thought more beautiful than another, it is that of harmonious operation; if there is one thought of greater solace to the mind than others, it is that of continual progress. And of all the arts, Music best illustrates this principle. She alone, not excepting her half-sister Poetry, feels most acutely the pulsations of the universe. She it is who in unison throbs with the beautiful and the vast. She hears the rhythm of everlasting law, and with sympathies boundless as space interprets the harmony of all things. She therefore is worthy to be the chorister of faith, hope and love, the trinity of man's emotions.

II.

CHINA.

FROM this introduction we pass to consider the growth and dissemination of the tonal art, and to estimate, if possible, its permeating and powerful influence upon the culture and morals of the human race. The triumphs of the art have been left for these latter ages, but it is impossible to point out any great nation which has been insensible to its power and charm.

How deep this influence, how powerful its charm, may be estimated by the consideration of nations which had their origin in the far-off ages of remote antiquity. There is perhaps no phase of thought so appealing in its sympathies, so laden with emotion, as that of reflection upon the efforts which culminate in a nation's civilization, in its advance towards the goal of social fraternity, in the opening of its purest minds to those great facts of universal life, those great principles of beauty, which, though some may think they belong to the abstract and immaterial, are the most real and abiding of all forces.

The poet feels this pathos as none other. He seems to hear the throb of the heart of humanity. There are borne to him strains of music from myriad souls, issuing from the ages which history records not. His eye beholds the first glimmerings of a nation's art, the passionate desire to attain the ideal, the beautiful, the earnest of all existence. And yet even more pathetic is the examination of a nation's art which has not fulfilled its promise, in which the vision of the beautiful, through various causes, has become distorted, and the artistic product grotesque—a satiric parody, as it were the mockings of an evil genius sporting with the principles of truth.

These remarks apply especially to the tonal art as developed in China and Hindustan. Both races, the Chinese and Hindus, loom upon our modern life through the mists of mythology. Both have histories so ancient that it is wellnigh impossible, if not quite, to unravel in their records the web of romance and of fact. Yet though so dissimilar in their mental characteristics, the genius of one exhausted in the most formal realism, the other in an unrestrained imagination, there is an alliance of musical theory, a correspondence in the artistic sense, or the want of it, which led to the omission of the tone B in their oldest scale of sounds. To both nations Nature appealed with wonderful and refreshing force. In both was enkindled a poetic sense which promised rich results. How appropriate, for instance, is the Chinese symbolism of things perfect and independent in the whole tones of the scales as heaven, sun, man; and of things imperfect and dependent in the half-tones as earth, moon, woman! That the Chinese possessed a keen musical instinct may be inferred from the additions to their oldest scale of five tones. This scale extended from F to D, omitting the B; but intellectual satisfaction demanded the insertion of E and B, the leaders and mediators, as they were termed, to F and C. The scale thus completed was still unable to satisfy their subtle feeling for tone, and sharps were added as intermediate half-tones to F, G, A, C, D, thus forming a chromatic scale of twelve semitones, as is our chromatic scale of to-day.

To theory a deep study and a large literature were devoted. Alone of the remote nations of antiquity, they possessed a system of octaves, a circle of fifths, and a normal tone, while each scale possessed a certain philosophical significance, showing that tone held an esteemed place in their conception and curriculum of education.

The whole of Chinese music was under the supervision of the State, and this is the cause of its non-advancement, of its falling short in such achievement as might naturally have been expected from the elaboration of its theory. Bureaucracy in China crushes all spontaneous effort. It leaves no freedom to the imagination, and allows in the most reluctant fashion any innovation. The past oppresses man's mind. A national consciousness has been attained, but the individual abrogates all the finer æsthetic instincts. The Chinese labour under too many disadvantages for their æsthetic sense to be thus fettered. It is with them a psychological impossibility to rise to a combination of ideas. Their language is agglutinative. In their writing every word requires a special sign; in their architecture the parts are independent, and not in harmony. Their musical instruments still further illustrate this incapacity for combination. They are, with few exceptions, instruments of percussion. Their popular melodies convey the same idea. They lack, as Naumann says, outline, form, and intrinsic merit, and are merely aimless wanderings among sounds. The best melodic specimens are their sacred songs, transmitted from time immemorial, and the songs of the people, sailors, and mountaineers. Thus, though Nature at first appealed strongly to the Chinese, though conceptions came to them of the deep significance of tone and the exalted nature of its mission; though throughout the Empire schools were established for its study and a literature devoted to its pursuit, yet the artistic, if not the theoretic, result was meagre and lifeless in the extreme. Their theory was far in advance of their practice, and shows a remarkable correspondence in its system of vibrations and intervals with the Pythagorean system of the ancient Greeks.

III.

HINDUSTAN.

FROM the rigid and conservative practice of China we pass to Hindustan, a land where imagination and phantasy bound with potent spell the minds of men.

A wonderful country geographically, with a variety of climes and rich profusion of products nowhere existent in any other single territory; the home of mystic theology, and of faiths held by the greater number of the human race; its classic language, Sanskrit, one of the most perfect vehicles of human thought; its literature the treasure-trove of modern scholars—is it not here that we might expect to find the permanent home and the most complete triumphs of the tonal art? Submerged by wave after wave of conquest, yet the distinctive characteristics of its numerous races are ineffaceable, and they trace their history to the fount of human thought and action.

As in the sister country of China, the music of Hindustan utters her first notes in the era of remote mythology. The art is the gift of the gods, and many are the narratives of its power and charm. In the Vedas—those sacred text-books of law and theology which so greatly influenced the Indian peoples—there are hymns specially designed for music, and the melodies to which they were set, Ragas, were supposed to possess miraculous powers. The Gandharven and Apsarasen too—performing genii and female dancers—were the especial creation of sages, and their mission was to minister to the delight of the gods and to tempt the probity of the recluse. In all things connected with the art the same luxuriant play of imagination prevails, the same utter disregard for natural explanation. Thus, each of the Gopis, shepherdesses and nymphs, of whom there were sixteen thousand, is said to have invented a new key, thus hoping by a distinctive melody to captivate and win the love of the young god Krishna. Their works on theory also bore extravagant titles, but their melodies, simple, ingenuous, and refreshing, were much more pleasing than the monotonous efforts of the Chinese.

The religious devotions of the Hindus called into existence a class of musicians devoted to the temple service, while another class was devoted to secular requirements. Both were known under the comprehensive title of Bayaderes, but the former alone, further distinguished as the 'Devadasi,' enjoyed social distinction. They were maidens free from all bodily defects, to whom their parents renounced all claim. If they married, their selection was limited to the highest caste, and their children, if daughters, were devoted to the temple service, and if sons, dedicated to the cult of musicians.

There were so many elements in Hindu life which, united, seemed so favourable for the advancement of music to a noble and permanent position, that we feel constrained to ask why, comparatively, it missed the realization. Two reasons present themselves. The unrestrained and fantastic imagination of the Hindu temperament failed through absence of persistence and the knowledge of right conditions and methods to embody the ideal before it, while another element, fatal to just art, lay in their over-refined and speculative philosophy. Hindu society, starting fundamentally from enlarged conceptions, and generous and humane laws, became in fact effete through the curse of unrestrained imagination.

IV.

EGYPT.

FROM Hindustan we pass to a no less remarkable land—a land which possesses for the historian profoundest interest. Belonging neither to the East nor West, Egypt formed a central home, the nucleus of ancient civilization. Indian, Assyrian, Phœnician, Hebrew, Persian, Greek, Roman, found here some attraction. Commerce and the arts abode here awhile. To it belongs in some measure the peculiar glory of fashioning the most supreme intellects, the moral Hebrew and the idealistic Greek—Moses and Plato. Learning, high polity, and morality were at Egypt's best periods the possessions of her upper classes. Caste prevailed, and foremost without a rival stood the priest, the embodiment of intellect and power. His capacities were undoubted, and philosophy and science owe to him no mean debt.

Secure from the fear of external oppression, Egypt tranquilly pursued her way, perfecting her civilization, and in her leisure allowed herself to reflect upon the phenomena and objects of life. The basis of her reflection was morality, and however much in her later history she declined from her first pure thought, yet the inhabitants of the Nile Valley were nurtured in religion. Nowhere, not even in ancient Israel, did the priestly hierarchy wield a more absolute authority; nowhere was such hierarchy possessed, considering the age and circumstances, of greater intellectual power.

This predominant religious feeling affected every phase of Egyptian life. The products of this thought are those strangely fascinating structures, the Pyramids, and those literal cities of the dead, the Theban and Memphian tombs, guarded by the symbolic Sphinx. Is it merely by contrast that the Sphinx, according to Egyptian thought representing the riddle of existence, is not far distant from Sinai? Is it merely a coincidence in the philosophy of history that from Egypt to Sinai, from Sinai to Calvary, is the course of profoundest thought, where aspiration, law, and love were each accorded its revelation?

The same restrictions that fettered the other arts in Egypt affected music in like manner. The pure joy of existence was to the Egyptian always tempered by the thought of coming judgment and reformatory tribulation. His art, though vast, was sober, his technique perfect, only the thing fashioned was suffused with symbolical allusion. Beauty for its own sake, perfected by the gift of grace—in other words, the fairest ideal of the sons of Greece, or the soul-illumined penetration of the Hebrew, abolishing all embodiment, and finding its sole satisfaction in contemplation of the moral attributes of God—the Egyptian just missed.

Thus, his music was not the pure joy of the one, nor the ecstatic expression of the other, though more nearly allied to the latter than the former. Concerning the actual system of the Egyptians we know little—indeed, less than of that of China or of Hindustan; but from the evidence supplied by the monuments of the number and variety of their instruments, it would appear they had advanced from childish practice to a system of orchestration and harmony.

As in other ancient nations, music was linked to the study of astronomy, and associated with the divinities. Their patron of song, Osiris, with the female singers who accompanied him, were metamorphosed by the Greeks into Phœbus Apollo and the Nine Muses. To their goddess Isis-Hathor, the Egyptians dedicated their most ideal conceptions. Plato bears evidence to the moral grandeur of their melodies, for he says: 'In their possession are songs having the power to exalt and ennoble mankind, and these could only emanate from gods and god-like men.' Herodotus, too, discovered in the melody of the

Egyptian Maneros (the beautiful lament of Isis on the death of Osiris) the Greek 'Linos.'*

Certain it is that music held honourable place in the refined and ceremonious civilization of the Nile Valley. The Egyptian grandee had attached to his court skilled musical performers, and the Egyptian priest was the ablest proficient upon the harp. The stately religious ceremonial of the Egyptians must likewise have made large demands for special cults of musicians. Whole classes of singers were devoted to the temple service, and thus through various agencies the art received encouragement.

On the tombs at El Amarna are to be seen representations of the instruments employed by the Egyptians. These are many, and comprise a complete orchestra. Harps, lyres, single and double flutes, hand kettledrums, and lutes. The most worthy and interesting of these is the harp, which is undoubtedly of Egyptian origin. In the early dynasties comparatively of simple structure, it had become a majestic and noble instrument at the culminating period of Egyptian civilization, about 1284 B.C. Its shape resembled that of the present day, the essential difference being that the front support was wanting.

The staid, reflecting character of the Egyptian would naturally lead him on to the study of harmony. His love of correspondence and explanation of natural phenomena, his scientific

* See Naumann.

analysis and moral insight, all would find sympathetic satisfaction in harmonic structure. The Egyptian melodies would appear to have floated within the limits of the tetrachord, limits admitting, and even compelling, a certain serenity and dignity of treatment. In the later dynasties the art of music was confined mostly to women, and the Persian invasion, 527-521 B.C., and ultimate contact with the Greeks, destroyed the essential characteristics of Egyptian music. Its glory, other than its own, is its influence upon the Hebrew and Greek forms of the art, and to these we now betake ourselves for consideration.

V.

ISRAEL.

WHEN Israel came out of Egypt the characteristics of the race were consummated: an intense individuality, patience against the most formidable obstacles, and a grand morality, which during their centuries of sojourn had been submitted to the most rigorous trials. The character of Abraham as the friend of God appeared in the nation he founded. Nature was felt to have a cause—that cause one holy omniscient Power in whom was no variableness nor shadow of turning. The innate quality of the Hebrew is prescience, and his mission was to open to men a moral kingdom, and make conscience the inquisitor of conduct.

The settlement of the first colony in Canaan with high moral aims naturally produced an exclusive character, and when Israel came to Egypt the policy of the Pharaohs intensified this characteristic. Joseph was the intermediary link to Moses, who, imbued with the intense spirit of his people and the knowledge of the Egyptians, needed that special communion with God in the desert to purify his every conception, and to embody in a code of inspired laws those principles of morality which have become the basis of conduct in highly civilized communities. Both nations had some things in common, both were of Semitic origin; but Moses knew from actual experience that the true knowledge of the Egyptian priest had become exclusive. The truths once taught by symbolism had, through so many centuries of highly organized and in part artificial civilization, become obscured. Symbolism had attained the greater importance. The future leader saw the perilous consequences, even to a nation's existence, of far-spreading symbolism, and the first of the commandments ran thus: 'Thou shalt have none other gods but Me.' Plastic art therefore was discouraged in Israel, but the natural emotions of a people must find expression.

The combined arts of poetry and music could alone satisfy the deep emotional temperament of the Hebrew, and minister to his moral aspirations. They alone could express his national exultation, sorrow for his shortcomings, and penitence for sin. Doubtless, the soothing influence of music had frequently calmed the troubled spirit of Israel under the tyranny of the Pharaohs, and the chief Egyptian instrument, the harp, was admirably adapted for this purpose.

The perturbed mind of Saul became amenable under its influence, while from the pictures drawn in the Psalms we may conclude it was the favourite national instrument.

The timbrel was another Egyptian instrument which was pressed into the service of the Israelites, and it will be remembered how Miriam, in the first of those grand songs, the impromptu outpouring of fervid gratitude and poetic genius, used the timbrel as an accompaniment. Among other women who were inspired with exalted song may be mentioned the daughter of Jephthah, and Deborah, and in later times the Virgin, whose beauteous chant the *Magnificat* is continuously arising from myriad hearts throughout Christendom.

We cannot trace in detail the evolution of musical service in the Temple, but we can see the broad results in its splendid celebration. The ordinances of Moses were added to from time to time, until in the reigns of David and Solomon music had become a great national art, and the subject of careful consideration.

The duty of electing proficient choristers devolved upon the Levites. These choristers were divided into numerous orders, each under the charge of an efficient master, and, as in other nations, they at length occupied a quasi-sacred position. In the Temple of Solomon it is probable that male choristers were alone engaged, but in the Second Temple female choristers took part. The singing was conducted in the antiphonal method, the method adopted at large by the Christian Church, and many of the psalms were constructed especially with regard to this method. In no ancient State was music the subject of such loftiness of aim and purity of treatment as in the Hebrew. Secular as well as sacred music was greatly encouraged, and David and Solomon are accredited with having formed bands of musicians and dancers who occupied a position somewhat analogous to that of our modern Court orchestra.

As the Greek poet and philosopher regarded the lyre as an instrument which would either compel or strengthen both song and wisdom, so the Hebrew prophets derived from the plaintive and emotional strains of the harp sweet stimulus and inspired moral utterance.

In the synagogues of Europe certain portions of the musical services indicate a survival of form through many centuries.

Although no positive evidence exists, yet argument deduces at least an interesting theory that the Hebrew melodies were confined within the limits of the tetrachord. The simple majesty of melodic movements within such limits is very impressive, and admirably adapted for religious requirements. The tetrachord and the scale of seven tones were the basis of Egyptian music, and with these, doubtless, the Hebrews were well acquainted. It seems hard to resist the conclusion that the Hebrews had not developed a system of harmony, but learned writers and musicians are at variance upon the point. Certainly, the deep spiritual need of the Hebrew, his insight and strength, his imperative need of expression, his noble penitence and soaring gratitude, all indicate a greater need than mere melodic outline could afford. But, be this as it may, the Hebrew genius was the first to exalt music to a position of absolute pre-eminence in the arts. It gave the first and worthy indications to which, but a century back, the great tone poets turned for guidance.

The history of the Hebrew, incomparably more than any other, has been counted worthy of the highest efforts of musical expression. His suffering and consolation, his triumph and despair, have been wrought into the minds of millions as an abiding spiritual force, both by the imperishable nature of his supreme moral power and intense genius, and by the nobly sustained interest of the great musicians, who have, with sublime song and epic, followed his efforts from the period of his sojourn in Egypt until the agonizing moment of the eclipse of his glory upon the cross at Calvary.

VI.

GREECE.

IN the course of our reflections upon the tonal art we have wandered from East to West. In China, India, Egypt, and Palestine we have listened to man's emotions striving for utterance. We have remarked the salient merits and defects which exalted and retarded the soaring spirit of harmony, and have particularly dwelt upon her influence in Egypt, her impassioned and sacred utterance in the Land of Israel. It is to this last-mentioned country, and one other not yet named, but whose influence is ever felt in every department of philosophy and art—namely, Hellas—that the modern West ever turns for inspiration and for guidance. The religious and intellectual qualities of Palestine and Hellas present the highest attainments of the human mind, for in whatever they have not respectively as nations excelled, yet it is either their influence or their history which has led to the noblest productions of modern genius. Indeed, for the modern world these are not defunct civilizations. They are vigorous and permeating, inseparably linked with national life.

But if Palestine is pre-eminent as a teacher of inspiring morality, Greece, in the realm of culture, holds undisputed sovereignty—a culture as abiding as the world of thought necessary to the needs of humanity—supplementing moral grace by intellectual and æsthetic beauty. Not that Greece was without religion. Plato was her priest, and Socrates her martyr, and previous to these great souls lit with the fire of ethereal virtue, in whom beauty was significant of all goodness both human and divine, the Greeks had a natural religion, which those who can comprehend it in the labyrinth of mythology will acknowledge to be very good; and for those who cannot, unaided, understand it, let them peruse Mr. Ruskin's matchless words concerning the goddess of earth, heart, and heaven—Athena.

The general characteristics of the early Greek mind are teachableness, receptivity, and a free, pure, and just imagination. Thus blessed with the primary elements of greatness, to which were added keen human sympathies, the nation came into contact with earlier and great civilizations, from which it extracted all that it could understand, making it the basis of enlarged and nobler principles; and that which it could not understand it wove into mythic beauty of fable and romance.

Egypt, Assyria, and Phœnicia lent their influence to mould the young nation's thought in morals, metaphysics, commerce, and art. These nations respectively laid the foundations upon which the Greek built his splendid fabric of art. Rude as were his first essays, yet they gave abundant promise, and his just imagination led him as he gazed upon the art of Egypt and Assyria to feel the void of beauty in the conservative practice of the one, and to consign to the sphere of decorative art the formal efforts of the other.

Phœnicia brought the gift of the alphabet, likewise the wares of conglomerated Egyptian and Assyrian art, and added that necessary stimulus to the Greek mind, to whose vision was opening the vista of ideal beauty.

It is a long way from the metopes of Selinus to the Acropolis, from the gorgon-headed Medusa to the consummation of plastic art in Phidias' statue of the Olympian Jove and Athena—a long way from the first rude bas-reliefs to the decorative frieze of the Parthenon, those marbles which are instinct with rhythmic grace and majesty, never falling short nor overstepping the boundaries of just art.

But while the plastic art was thus approaching its perfect form, an art linked with that of music, poetry, had from its first mighty source in Homer developed from epic to lyric, thence to tragedy, comedy, and the drama. These forms of composition, invented by the Greek genius, have rarely been equalled, and never excelled, save perhaps by our immortal Shakespeare.

Thales, too, was the founder of a distinguished line of natural philosophers, upon whose foundation of thought the moderns have erected their temple of science. History had a worthy founder in Herodotus, painting in Cimon of Cleonæ; while in architecture the Greeks were without a rival, evolving from the first rude outlines of their primitive dwellings in Asia Minor those splendid temples in the construction of which were used consecutively the Doric, Ionic, and Corinthian columns.

A civilization so wonderful and productive needed to enhance its beauty but virtue and love. Socrates and Plato added these, the one testifying thereto by his death, the other by his soul-inspired writings.

Having thus briefly considered the arts in which the Greeks were pre-eminent, let us turn to that of music, bearing in mind that it was to poetry, as painting to statuary, subsidiary. It was one of the arts reserved for recent time to develop and perfect; but herein is the glory of Greece, that it has been developed and perfected upon the basis of her treatment.

Before entering upon the historical study of Greek music, it will be profitable and interesting to reflect upon the ideas associated with the art in Greek mythology. These ideas are presented to us through fables, but we can at least try to catch the spirit of the traditions, which are pregnant with instructive meaning. Indeed, the key of the Greek mind is to be discovered in mythology. We see here beautiful symbolism, loving converse with Nature, and that guileless expression of natural emotion which in a young nation, as in a young child, is a healthful and hopeful symptom. The Greek loved the world— it was to him very fair. The sunshine, brook and stream, mountain, grove, and ocean, the winged breath of heaven and the o'er-arching sky, the clear firmament and the radiant stars—these were his instructors. Melody was in his heart, and the real and the abstract were dealt with by him in simple fashion. Who would banish this refreshing simplicity from the pages of young humanity? rather, is it not to us very sweet, as the voices of children at play chanting the pastoral of perpetual youth?

The old Greeks were heroic children. Cannot we picture the expedition of the Argonauts, the beautiful Athena superintending the building of the *Argo?* Cannot we hear the plash of the oars, and see the feathered spray glinting in the sunlight as the band of heroes depart in search of the golden fleece? And then, when danger came upon them, what more natural than that Orpheus—he to whom Apollo and the muses had entrusted the lyre, and he who subsequently subdued by his melodies even the pains of Hades, and won his way to the presence of his beloved Eurydice—should have cheered their hearts with music? This same Apollo, too—Apollo Musagetes—the patron of music, what mythic fables of romance and beauty are not woven around him! And the nine muses, amongst whom were Euterpe, Erato, and Terpsichore, the muses of the tonal art and dance, and Polyhymnia, the muse of the sublime hymn! It was from Apollo that the Homeric bards derived the art of song, while, concerning the muses, were not their favourite haunts by the sacred fountains of Aganippe and Hippocrene, by Mount Parnassus and the Castilian spring? Does not all this signify the song of poesy and Nature? Dionysus, god of the vine, representing the intoxicating power of Nature, was another mythic personage, from whose worship arose the Bacchanalian orgies and the subsequent Greek drama. The sirens, too, who endeavoured to allure the Argonauts, are representative of the seductive powers of sensuous tone. Thus we see how music is interwoven with the dawning life of the ancient Greeks.

Passing by the period of mythology, we enter into the historical period for music about 676 B.C. The occasion is the second Messenian war, when the Spartans, dismayed by the valour of their opponents, sent for advice to the Delphic oracle, who bade them apply to Athens for a leader. Tyrtæus was therefore sent, and succeeded, by the enthusiasm which he aroused by his martial songs, in reviving the courage of the Lacedæmonians.

We may, however, consider Terpander as the first Greek musician of solid renown. His genius materially affected Greek poetry, giving great impetus to the lyric form in which the young nation, after the decay of epic minstrelsy, embodied its aspirations. The lyric poems were sung on festive occasions to the accompaniment of a musical instrument, and it was in the composition of these melodic accompaniments that Terpander won renown. His creations had exercised a beneficent influence over the Spartan youth, and among the Lacedæmonians he was held in high esteem.

The Lesban school, which included the distinguished names of Arion, Alcæus and Sappho, was founded by him; while he added three additional strings to the lyre and invented a new notation.

Concerning Arion there is a beautiful myth illustrating the power of melody. He had successfully carried away the prizes at a musical contest in Sicily, whither he had gone from the Court of Periander at Corinth. His treasures were coveted upon his return journey by the sailors, who intended his destruction. Prevailing upon them to allow him once again to touch the strings of his beloved lyre, he invoked the gods with sweetest melody, and cast himself into the sea. The dolphins playing around the ship were enchanted, and one of them bore the musician upon his back to Corinth.

Thus is fabled the power of music over the brute creation; and, furthermore, the Greeks, with that fit sense which so distinguished them, perpetuated the memory of Arion by naming after him a constellation of the stars.

In the compositions of Arion we see yet again the influence of music upon the sister art of poetry. He is said to have invented the Dithyramb, from which subsequently sprang the sublime production of the tragic muse at Athens.

Of the two remaining members of the Lesban school, there is a vase in the Munich Museum on which is depicted the contest between Alcæus and Sappho. The former is accompanying himself upon the lyre, and from this mode of accompaniment is derived the term of lyric poet.

Concerning Sappho, we have a charming picture of her as Queen of Culture. The foremost of Greek poetesses, she excelled in lyric form, and is accredited with the invention of a new instrument, the barbiton. Around her at Mytilene were gathered noble maidens, whom she instructed in the arts of poetry, song, and dance. There remain to us representations of these maidens playing upon the lyre, and their rhythmic grace and movements are indicative of that pure joy of existence so happily, and even pathetically, felt by the Greeks.

In this first school we have seen how far-reaching, and of what magnitude, was the influence of music upon the future form of poetry and the drama, and Tisias, the contemporary of Arion, who was the director of the chorus, effected its diversion into three parts, called strophe, antistrophe, and epodus. A few years later a master mind was to investigate and formulate the theory of Greek music.

In Pythagoras we have an example of that comprehensive, reflective, and creative character which enabled the Greeks to build up their systems of philosophy and science. He was a native of Samos, and, desirous of knowledge, visited Egypt and Babylon. Contact with Egypt had bestowed or quickened a lofty ideal of human life. His deep reflections upon the spiritual relation of man's character to the Godhead ally him in thought to Plato. His lofty enthusiasm, and the exalted character of his teaching, attracted the noblest of the families of Greece. Various brotherhoods were formed throughout Magna Græcia, and for some time it seemed that the intellectual and political power of the Pythagoreans would dominate the life of Hellas.

But this was not to be. The basis of Pythagorean philosophy was harmony governed by numerical laws. All movements in Nature were to him harmonical. His attentive ear caught the distant music of the spheres, which was associated by him in a symbolical manner with the seven notes of the scale. He likewise, with the later

Arabian philosophers, discerned the beneficent effects of music upon a deranged intellect, and his disciples at morn and even ever prepared and refreshed themselves by performances upon the lyre.

Leaving these abstract conceptions, we descend to undoubted scientific achievement. 'Pythagoras discovered the numerical relation of one tone to another,' 'fixing the ratio of the tonic to the octave as 1 to 2, the tonic to its fifth as 2 to 3, the tonic to the fourth as 3 to 4, and, on account of the numerical simplicity of the ratio of these three intervals, pronounced them perfect musical consonances.'* Furthermore, Pythagoras is said to have perfected the scale of Terpander by adding an eighth note, supplying the omission by the fifth note, B, of the Doric scale.

It may be interesting to remark here the estimation in which the primary scales of Greece were held. The two ancient scales were the Doric and the Phrygian. Later the Lydian was introduced from Asia Minor. We perceive at once in the Doric scale the same qualities of mind as those prominent in Doric architecture — a simple ideal strength and beauty. The teachers of the Spartan youth expressly advocated this scale as the vehicle of inspiring all the higher qualities of mind.

Music was taken seriously in Greece. The greatest of her philosophers entered into momen-

* Naumann.

tous discussions upon the moral effects of tone. Plato condemned the Lydian scale as infusing qualities opposite to those mentioned. On the other hand, Aristotle discerned in it the power of awakening the love of modesty and purity, and the same philosopher also ascribed to the Phrygian the power of evoking inspiration. Counterpoint was unpractised. This, Gothic architecture and painting, were to be the supreme forms of expressive joy reserved for a new and true form of faith—Christianity.

We are now approaching that period of the intellectual, moral, and æsthetic achievements of the Greek mind which has cast its potent and enchanting spell over the whole of human history. The spirit of Greek manhood had well-nigh reached its culminating excellence, was being moulded by various elements for that momentous contest which was to decide whether the West was to be nurtured in liberty, to reach the goal of its aspirations, or to be steeped in the enervating sensuality, to succumb to the cruel and cynical laws, of the East. The heart yet thrills at the mention of Marathon. We feel, even now, the strife of that conflict, the tumultuous joy of that victory.

For about three-quarters of a century before that memorable event, the drama, supported by music, was striving to find its most perfect utterance. Both tragedy and comedy were of Doric origin, and arose out of the worship of Dionysus, and tragedy was the offspring of the dithyrambic odes, with which that music was associated. We have seen what great influence the genius of Arion exerted upon tragedy by his elaboration of the dithyramb, which was sung under his direction by a chorus of fifty specially trained persons. These songs were accompanied by gestures which, in the time of Pisistratus, suffered innovation under Thespis, who introduced an actor for the purpose of giving rest to the chorus. Thespis himself gave the first representation, sustaining the dialogue with the chorus. These dialogues were delivered in recitative, the chorus supplying the melody, though even the dialogue was accompanied by musical instruments.

Thus was the commencement of the Greek drama. Nobly moulded by the genius of Æschylus, who gave special prominence to the musical accompaniments, it attained its highest perfection in the creations of Sophocles, who somewhat curtailed the musical portions by the introduction of a third actor. Hence it passed to Euripides, and subsequently declined.

Now that music, in conjunction with the drama, was employed to express the emotions incidental to the subject treated, it at once becomes apparent that the art had freed itself from the conventionality of religious exercises. True, in Greece it was ever the handmaid of poetry. The great bards and poets used it to supplement their recitations and creations, but, nevertheless, during the administration of Pericles it made great advances towards an independent position.

Brilliant and successful as the administration of Pericles proved for promoting the various forms of art, yet his foreign policy, dictated by a pride which lacked the necessary material support for its attainment, ultimately led to the irretrievable ruin of the Athenian State. But before the glory of Athens was to pale, there arose in its moral firmament two twin souls, whose light was kindled by the Holy Spirit— Socrates and Plato, master and disciple. In these was consummated all that was noblest of Hellas.

Not far distant was Bethlehem. Plato was the morning star before the rising sun. Hear what he says concerning music:

'The soul which has seen most of truth shall come to the birth as a philosopher, or artist, or *musician* or lover.'

Yes! the artist had come to the birth, and had reached fairest manhood. Phidias wrought in marble the ideal beauty Plato expressed in words. The philosopher had come to the birth, and was well grown. The lover in Socrates and Plato had clasped their Lord of truth. But Music? Yes, she had come to the birth; but before she arose in her lofty majesty, to pour forth those mighty tone epics, the utterance and glory of this modern age, there were to be kindled new hopes and aspirations for man. Ancient political systems were to die, new systems to be born, and now in these later days music stands supreme in art, and with unshaken faith and volume of soaring song declares that the Redeemer liveth.

That music was destined for this high position might have been predicated from Plato's criticism upon the functions of the art. Disdaining the idea that it was merely to minister to the gratification of the senses, he showed that by eliminating all that was fantastic, effeminate and lascivious, and preserving that which was pure, firm and dignified, it was a most valuable influence in the education of the nation; and Aristotle in the main confirmed the ideas of his great master. Aristoxenus, 350 B.C., a philosopher who likewise investigated the nature of music, was opposed to the theory of Pythagoras, deducing all tones from numerical ratio. He rather trusted to the ear. Hence his followers were called Harmonists; those of Pythagoras, Canonists.

But already Music had fallen from her high estate. We see a similar decline in the drama and statuary. From the majesty and ideal beauty of Phidias we pass to Praxiteles' somewhat dreamy and effeminate productions. From Sophocles we pass to Euripides, and then to less worthy successors. The real cause of the decline in art was the decline in morals. The names associated with music in this decline are Euclid, Diodorus, Plutarch, and Nicomachus.

Let us now dwell for a short time upon the musical instruments employed by the Greeks.

The chief instruments were the lyre and flute; and although, as we have seen, their invention is attributed to Apollo, yet they were, without doubt, introduced into Greece from Asia and Egypt. The lyre was the precursor of several stringed instruments. Nearest in relation to it stood the cithar, chiefly used by the bards and virtuosi. The lyre was the favourite instrument of the general public. Then there was the psalter, or long lyre, the chelys and tregon—all similar stringed instruments. These were played by the plectrum or fingers, and never by the bow. Of the wind instruments, the flute was the most important. Then came the trumpet, horn, and syrinx. The flute was chiefly used in religious services; but it rather resembled the oboe or clarionet than the modern instrument of the same name. The tympanum (hand-drum) and cymbalum (kettle-drum) were used in the Bacchanalian orgies.

Both Plato and Aristotle attached great importance to the kind of instruments to be used. The latter especially recommended the genuine Hellenic lyre of eight strings. Those instruments which lent themselves merely to digital skill he severely condemned.

With these remarks we conclude our survey of Greek music.

THE EARLY CHRISTIAN AND MIDDLE AGES.

VII.

THE ADVENT OF THE SPIRIT OF LOVE.

AT the decline of the intellectual, moral, and æsthetic power of Greece a veil of darkness seems to have fallen upon the classic age. True, the Romans established a world-wide empire, and true, the fabric was built up by the individual through a sense of duty subordinating himself to the welfare and glory of the State. But in the realm of thought and expression, whether upon the constituent elements of Nature and the laws for the government thereof, or in that realm where morality and beauty sought satisfaction for the never-to-be-subdued yearnings of the soul, the Romans acknowledged the supremacy of Greece. For a time the world saw in the young commonwealth a splendid example of chastity and temperance, but the utilitarian mind of the Roman became vulgarized by material achievement. When ambition, directed by the genius of statesmanship, had gained an empire, an unparalleled luxury slowly but surely performed its disintegrating work, and the mind of the latter-day Roman, reflecting upon his worldwide possessions, playing for vast stakes by the dice of intrigue, weary with care, asked of one who had arisen in his dominions of the nature of truth. Through many centuries and in many climes had this question been oft repeated. The soul had seen visions of truth. Indian, Egyptian, Jew, Greek, testify to this, but the vision was obscured, and the truth could not be attained. Elaborate systems, sprung from whatever beautiful conceptions, could not attain truth, for truth in its nature is simple and single-minded. It is the perfect correspondence of the soul with God. All Nature must be evolving to this truth, because its laws are in accordance with the purpose of God, whose mind bestowed them. But man, the child and the noblest production of God, how shall he attain truth? Even through the vision of God made manifest in Love. To the intellectual and moral force which the genius and inspiration of the pre-Christian world had left as legacy to its successors there was to be added the element of Divine love to complete the educational influence of the forces mentioned, directing them by the pure motives which love alone could supply, and in which alone they could be clothed with highest honour.

The opportuneness of the moment for this revelation in the person of Christ has been acknowledged by the supporters and detractors of the faith He founded. The achievements of the human race, beautiful and necessary as they had been, could not supply the answer to that profound question of the Roman Governor, 'What is truth?' The soul of humanity was waiting for the advent of its Lord, and although for the moment it knew Him not, yet, but a few years, and the impulse it had received gathered irresistible power and founded a new kingdom—the kingdom of perfect love—which, overstepping the boundaries of race and creed, was to be immortal. At last the vision of poet, prophet, and philosopher was realized. At last man stood in the presence of the Father. Transfigured by a new glory, filled with emotions which impelled expression, through what medium could they most freely flow? Could they receive expression and idealization after the vision of Phidias or of Plato? Could Homer or the tragedies of Sophocles supply the form of art which would most aptly relieve the overburdened soul? No! The plastic art of Greece, incomparable in its sphere, however blended with ideal dignity and strength, was yet but individual. It could not symbolize to any appreciable extent the fervid emotions which the Gospel of Love called most passionately into being. The epic and the drama, indeed, were capable of expressing far more aptly the emotions and hopes of man, but even here the former presupposes for its appreciation a high standard of culture not likely to be attained by the multitude, and the latter, though more pictorial, cannot deal for the individual with the fleeting play of light and shadow in the Christian life. Moreover, at the commencement of the Christian era the gladiatorial display was barbarous compared to the educational and moral influence exerted by the profound thought and beauty of the Greek drama. The drama had suffered temporary banishment, and could not serve as a model. There remained two arts, both in comparative infancy—music and painting—which were destined to be the media of the new ideal before the souls of men. To these, some six centuries later, was added the Gothic form of architecture, chastened with aspiration, purity, and love.

Concerning two of these arts—painting and Gothic architecture—we see that they are more restricted, because more definite, than music. Successful as the painter may be in portraying for a moment intensity of feeling, and even by grouping and composition showing the gradual development of an idea to its highest form, yet it never in this respect can be compared with that of the tonal art. The latter, affording subtlest analysis to the feelings, feels, as it were, almost as keenly as the imagination the various phases which lead to the ultimate expression, whether it be the severely ideal, the tempestuously passionate, or the majesty of broad and general treatment. This is by reason of the co-extensive sympathy which music has with the laws of the physical and moral world. The three forms of Christian art afford an admirable illustration of the evolution of the beautiful in the realm of feeling. We cannot trace here the growth of painting and Gothic architecture, but the world will probably never know how much it is indebted for all that it holds hallowed in womanhood to those sublime parables of motherhood and chastity depicted with such serenity and pathos by the sympathetic genius of Raphael. Neither does the world reflect how much it owes to those aspirations of nameless workers which are perpetuated in the soaring unity of Gothic arch and column.

But when these arts had reached their highest expression, when the pressing needs of humanity required yet a deeper expression, Music, of slower growth than any other art, assembled all her forces, and with allied sympathy with the remote and near, with Nature's song and the far-off vibration of heavenly harmony in the soul, feeling as no other art had done the impulse of Christianity, she burst into immortal epic and sweetest song of hope and love. By her nature she alone in art was fated to be the most perfect exponent of the universal Gospel of Love. We have seen of old that her voice was always sweeter when chanting in the Temple choir, and now, not only in the cathedral, but in the home, she dispels the cares of day by refreshing weary souls with mirth, or leads them into the sanctuary of peace. And, moreover, if, for want of a better word, we speak of her achievements in the secular realm of art, where shall we find such perfect expression of dignity, grace, strength, passion, and pathos as afforded in the sonatas of Beethoven? With these in its keeping and for its glory, the modern world fears no comparison of genius and inspiration with the noblest production of the golden age of Greece. Let us endeavour, then, to trace this evolution, to catch the spirit of her minstrelsy.

VIII.

MUSIC AND THE EARLY CHURCH.

THE development of music for the next ten centuries was intimately associated with the Christian Church. It was pre-eminently the art of consolation and of healing, qualified as no other to minister to the new faith in the hour of direst need, and to chant triumphant exultation in the hour of universal triumph. The latter time, however, was far distant yet. Christianity came into conflict with the religious and political system of Rome, and fierce enmity ensued. In the depths of forests and in the Catacombs, the sustaining power of music fortified the resolution of the Christian converts, and one of the first martyrs, St. Cecilia, became its patron saint. St. Augustine, too, was wooed by its sweet influence, and in the first two centuries it was a growing power in the Christian service.

Of a necessity, the early Christians adopted for the expression of their emotions the art forms around them, but in the second century there dawned in the minds of men that beautiful conception of a universal Church, in which the sons of men and the brethren of the Son of God should draw near in loving communion with the Father. Such a conception naturally widened and strengthened the influence of the art we are considering. An attempt was made to provide a common hymnology for Christendom, which, under Constantine and his mother, Helena, found fulfilment, and the erection of magnificent churches led to the appointment of choirs specially trained for the performance of the services. To aid in this development, a singing school was established by St. Sylvester in Rome, and in the expiring years of the fourth century original hymns were introduced, which were probably a strain of poetry independent of all tradition. SS. Chrysostom and Cyprian likewise exerted their influence for the admission of new melodies, but it was reserved for St. Ambrose to establish for two centuries the future form of Church music.

His system was presumably analogous to that of the Greeks, the tone being subordinate to the metrical character of the text, and it was this form of chant which so deeply affected St. Augustine, and which, as the future Bishop of Hippo, he introduced into Northern Africa. It was at the end of the fourth century, too, that St. Ephraim is supposed to have invented the Neume notation (from Greek *pneuma*, a breathing), a system of signs which indicated to the priest ' the

Music and the Early Church

inflexions and modulations required in the declamation of the Gospel, Epistle, and Psalms.' But it was the genius of Gregory the Great which did so much to enlarge and establish musical art. When, at the end of the sixth century, he ascended the Papal chair, he resolved to promote a canonical method of musical service which should not only minister to the satisfaction of the people, but which, adopted universally, should ensure harmony of spirit and design, and by the exclusion of incongruous elements tend to solidify the component parts of Christendom.

His efforts were eminently successful, and the greater freedom which music consequently enjoyed had a powerful and far-reaching influence upon the future independence of the art. Gregory also added four scales, known as 'plagal,' to the hitherto existing Ambrosian authentic scales, and to perpetuate his system founded a musical academy at Rome. This soon became famous, and singers were invited from, or sent to, England, France, and Switzerland. He likewise arranged the Mass, the source of so many inspiring compositions, as it now exists, and, indeed, much of the Gregorian music is still preserved in the Roman Catholic ritual. The broad effect of Gregory's reform was to make the tone independent of the text, whereas in the Ambrosian chant it had been subordinate.

Charlemagne, too, greatly facilitated the dissemination of the Gregorian method by founding singing schools in various cities of the empire, and it was likewise about this time that instrumental music received great encouragement. The organ, known to the nations of antiquity, was greatly perfected by the Byzantines, who introduced it into Germany. From thence it was imported into Italy, and subsequently into England and France, for use in Divine service. But in the first ten centuries stringed instruments were in the ascendant. These included the rotte and rebab, psalteries and harps. The two first-mentioned are by far the most interesting, as it was from their combination that the stringed instruments of to-day—violins, basses, etc.—have evolved.

We have already spoken of the notation invented by St. Ephraim. Naturally, the system underwent many modifications by his successors, until, in the fourteenth century, we see clearly foreshadowed our present system of five-lined staves. It is impossible to praise too highly the genius and perseverance of the Roman Catholic Fathers and monks in the cause of music. A long line of distinguished names shows how faithfully they laboured to render the art worthy to express the deep emotions of the soul, and the productions they have left illustrate the peculiar genius and the mental characteristics of the age in which they lived. For not a little of the highest form of Church music are we indebted to such monks as Notker Balbulus of the monastic school of St. Gall, the famed Prior St. Bernard of Clairvaux,

Thomas of Celano and Jacopone, and the celebrated St. Thomas Aquinas. Other illustrious names are those of Hucbald and Guido of Arezzo. To both we are under deep obligations for their indefatigable labours in the dissemination of part-singing, and to the latter for his system of solmization. Moreover, as one movement in art leads to another, so the practice of part-singing necessitated a mensural system, the measurement of notes into proper values and bars. Franco of Cologne, a celebrated teacher who lived in the latter part of the twelfth century, was the vigorous exponent of this method, and his system of harmony was similar to that of the present day. He was distinguished likewise for his advocacy of part-singing in contrary motion, which is, of course, the true and most harmonious method.

IX.

THE TROUBADOURS AND MINNESINGERS.

WHILE the Church was thus exercising a powerful influence over certain forms of musical art, there was growing up amongst the people an increasing love of melody without regard to any definite form, yet undoubtedly supplying a correlative mood of brightness, freedom, and grace, the outcome of natural emotion, to the more serious perceptions and aims which were necessarily embodied in sacred songs. The two movements were requisite for the ultimate triumph of the tonal art.

Charlemagne, to whom, as we have seen, we are indebted on other grounds, collected, without prejudice, the heroic songs and sagas of the heathen Germans, and the forms of folk-song were carried from province to province, from country to country, by the wandering minstrels, a class occupying the lowest social status, and to whom the protection of the law and the sympathy of the Church were alike denied. This class was known by different names in different countries,

The Troubadours and Minnesingers 49

and it has been plausibly urged that these strollers were the descendants of the old Roman gladiators and comedians, who, upon the disruption of the Roman Empire, were cast adrift to gain a livelihood amongst strange peoples by the exercise of their wits. Certain it is that there was a romantic strain in their disposition, but by their tact and skill they ingratiated themselves into the favour of those classes who at first so cruelly oppressed them, so that eventually they were allowed to perform their sacred plays, seasoned with allusions and wit of the time, in the interiors of the churches.

These mountebanks and strolling minstrels were likewise employed by the troubadours and minnesingers as instrumental accompanists, but their talent was such, and their performances so excellent upon the rota, rebeck, lute, and fife, that the troubadours forsook their indolent attitude, and devoted themselves to attaining a like proficiency.

These circumstances greatly aided the dissemination of musical taste in the Middle Ages. We find, too, that the troubadours were quick to recognise the poetic and melodic gifts of the Provençal people, and they adapted their lays, giving to them a nobler language and improved melody. The compositions of these courtly musicians were canzonets, servantes, tenzone, roundelays, and pastourelles, and in them they forsook the old Church modes and used our modern major and minor keys.

As Naumann truly says, this innovation paved the way for the final secession of art music in the seventeenth century from the Church modes to the adoption of our modern system of scales and keys. Moreover, during the twelfth and thirteenth centuries attempts were made in part-writing, and harmony and counterpoint were foreshadowed.

In Spain the troubadours were known as 'trobadores,' and in England as 'minstrels.' The Crusades naturally had a great effect upon every phase of life in the Middle Ages. The tide of emotional chivalry widened the sympathies of the various classes, and helped to break down the barriers of absolutism. We have already remarked upon the introduction of instruments of Eastern origin into Western Europe, and the mental electricity of the time conveyed an interchange of melody and song.

From the troubadours we pass to the minnesingers, who became eminent in Germany from about the middle of the twelfth century. Abandoning to some extent the courtly songs of the troubadours, they entered rather into those subjects which lay nearer to the heart of the people, thus giving to poetry a more feeling and elevated tone. Some of their compositions are undoubtedly pathetic and beautiful, embracing moral, religious, and poetical topics.

Unlike the troubadours, they often improvised

The Troubadours and Minnesingers

both lays and music, and those who excelled in this species of composition were termed meistersingers. The transition from the minnesong to the meistersong in the fourteenth century had an important bearing upon the future of music. The latter would seem to have originated in Mayence, and from thence spread to the principal cities of Germany.

By this transition the study of music passed from the classes previously mentioned to the city burghers. Guilds were established, and the laws which governed them imposed a certain restraint upon the free development of the art. The meistersong flourished until about the end of the seventeenth century, when it commenced to decay.

X.

THE EARLIEST FRENCH SCHOOL.

IN taking leave of minstrelsy, as practised by the trouvères, troubadours, and minnesingers, we retrace our steps, and enter, as regards culture, the most famous city of Western Europe. Becoming the capital of France at the commencement of the sixth century, Paris early illumined the surrounding countries with her intellectual rays and vivid genius. Ever a centralizing force, she gathers, as it were by a law of intellectual gravitation, the master spirits of the ages. The foundation of her celebrated University gave her a powerful and far-reaching influence upon European thought. The streams of knowledge both united and diverged at Paris, and united with knowledge were the beautiful in form and the truthful in conception, so that the mediæval mind, striving to embody its peculiar ideal, created the Gothic arch in architecture and polyphony in music.

The Crusades had given a powerful impetus to the intellect of Europe. Men began to reflect upon the various problems presented by Nature,

The Earliest French School

but Christianity still held up as highest ideal the union of tenderness and love. Thus, the East gave both the intellectual and the ideal, and was it not the fusion of these two forces which was productive of harmony in the arts? for diverse forms, separately beautiful, attain a more profound and spiritual significance when harmonized in one perfect conception. The Gothic is the visible embodiment of the peculiar mental and spiritual forces of life in the early Middle Ages, and although not at first so quickly and gloriously manifest, being more ethereal and difficult to weld into a complete art, we can securely trace the evolution of the characteristics previously mentioned in the final attainment of the government of tone by harmonious laws.

The influence of the two arts was considerable one upon the other. At the moment when the Cathedral of Notre Dame was projected, a musical school was established in Paris, whose masters were closely associated with the cathedral services, and when the great Cathedral of Cologne was rising, Franco, of the same city, consciously or unconsciously, was moulding the same forces into definite expression in music. We have to tender our gratitude to a long line of Churchmen for the individual efforts which culminated in the foundation of this first musical school.

From the days of Hucbald and Guido men had striven to attain harmony in song, to express the subtle yearnings of the soul in pathetic melody, and though, to our modern ears, their methods were harsh and dissonant, yet they are not on that account to be lightly esteemed. The practice which prevailed amongst choristers of adding melodic embellishments to the cantus firmus, or fixed chant, likewise aided the mental movement, which was at length to evolve a refined, powerful, and glorious art, governed by appropriate laws.

Counterpoint, at first practised in Paris, was the first link in the chain of evolution. It arose inevitably from the method of singing termed descantus. The cantus firmus consisted of measured notes, to which a counterpart was added, free and independent in movement, and which, harmonized with the melody, could alone give the heart and understanding the same sense of unity as that afforded in the diverging and uniting columns of the Gothic.

The French genius quickly added other forms to the double, viz., the triple and the quadruple. In the triple, or triplum, the composer had the choice of three methods, viz., the motette, which is distinguished by allowing each voice a different text; the rondeau, a secular composition evolved by the Paris school from folk-music; and the conduit, consisting of two, three, or four parts, likewise secular, which would appear to have been written for instrumental purposes.

Moreover, in the compositions of the period by Perotin, Walter Odington, and Jean de Garlande, we meet with such forms as imitation, canon,

The Earliest French School

and double counterpoint, forms ultimately carried to the highest perfection by the genius of Sebastian Bach. Several valuable treatises likewise emanated from the masters of the Paris school, concerning both theory and performance.

To Franco of Paris, as well as Franco of Cologne, we are much indebted for the improvement of the mensural song. The latter master was the disciple of the former, and a long line of eminent names adorns this first and noble school, which enjoyed existence for nearly three hundred years, bringing to the birth, meanwhile, the Gallo-Belgic and the Netherland, which now claim our attention.

XI.

THE GALLO-BELGIC SCHOOL.

FROM Paris we pass to Flanders and the Netherlands, and in the working of the Gallo-Belgic and Netherland schools will be traced yet further the evolution of form in music, the strivings of earnest minds for mastery over tone, and the endeavour to make their art the vehicle of varied and exalted expression.

The inhabitants of Flanders were deeply sensitive to tonal effect. It was thence that the Sacred Organum of Hucbald spread into the neighbouring territories, an initiatory movement in the art of part-singing, which, as we have seen, the French genius admirably utilized, so that there sprang from it the forms of harmonic writing. This love of the art impelled pilgrimages from Flanders to Paris, so that those who were students became masters, and, leaving the confines of Paris and their native territories, became great teachers in foreign countries.

The Netherland school is especially distinguished by the generous love with which its

The Gallo-Belgic School

apostles laboured, but before considering this school we will turn our attention to the Gallo-Belgic, the connecting-link between the French and the Netherland institutions.

The most celebrated master of the Gallo-Belgic school was Dufay; but immediately preceding him was Zeelandia, who laboured 'to abolish the unpleasant perfect consonances of the Greeks, especially the tedious and monotonous fourths, fifths, and octaves,'* and who in his writings endeavoured to substitute for these intervals the 'hitherto sparingly-used thirds and sixths.'

The genius of Dufay quickly discerned the valuable qualities of folk-music, qualities of ease, grace, and melody, which the music of the Church, owing to conservative and pedantic practice, so sadly lacked. In the Masses which Dufay wrote he substituted for the cantus firmus popular melodies; indeed, both melody and text were borrowed from the people. This practice of appropriation was extensively and persistently resorted to by the masters of the Gallo-Belgic and Netherland schools.

Dufay discarded likewise the use of parallel fifths, used by previous writers, and further adopted the open note style. But, more important in the evolution of the art, he initiated the purest style of canonic part-writing, using imitation throughout his compositions. Like a true poet, he would not sacrifice the spirit to the

* Naumann, p. 306.

letter, and, while respecting law, would not yield his individuality. Euphonic beauty, scientifically expressed, was the aim and attainment of this master.

The efforts of Dufay were worthily supplemented by those of Antoine de Busnois, born in Flanders, 1440 A.D. His songs exhibit a marked improvement upon those of the earlier masters. Without sacrificing euphony, he rendered science a more obedient servant. This trait is specially discernible in his canonic treatment, which is more continuous than Dufay's. He was also superior as a harmonist, and a striking feature in his compositions is the resolution of the seventh tone. With this master the pre-eminence of the Gallo-Belgic school ceased; but we have seen how fruitful were its labours, how important its euphonic workings.

XII.

THE NETHERLAND SCHOOL.

IN the French and Gallo-Belgic schools we have watched Music gradually and patiently divest herself of the old Church forms—have seen her with new delight express herself in more natural melodies, have seen her also with the calm vision of balanced genius endeavour to assimilate melody to correct law, and thus produce a perfect art. Untiringly, unceasingly, music progressed from stage to stage, and at the rise of the Netherland school upon the teaching of the French and Gallo-Belgic we see what forces had gathered, how earnest the desire for the controlling force of law, which the centuries immediately preceding had generated.

A long and honoured list of names testifies to the enduring influence of the Netherland school. Its masters were zealous in the cause of art, and their labours and journeyings were sustained by love. In the fifteenth century the Netherlands was the home of song. Melody was in the hearts of the people, and such was the renown the Netherland choristers had attained, that they were in great request in foreign States.

The masters with whom we meet are men of large and comprehensive minds. Analysis, creativeness, and a sense of the beautiful characterize their works. The foundation of their labour was conscientiousness, enlarged by spirituality. This was the mission of the North, and it was essential that the mighty fabric of modern music should rest upon such sure foundations. Intellectual vivacity and sensual charm could enter as constituent elements at a later period, but intensity of purpose, the mental characteristic of the North, was at first the most requisite quality.

The founder of the Netherland school was Okeghem, born between 1425 and 1430, and a number of gifted pupils gathered round him. The bias of Okeghem's mind was scientific, and his large and comprehensive faculties enabled him to gather up the scattered elements of the art, and to evolve therefrom the canon and fugatic modes of writing. It was this mastery over technical forms which enabled the Netherland masters to raise music to such high estate. Hitherto individuals had worked with no reference to the efforts of others. They had seen the ideal before them, but knew not how to attain it.

But the school with which we are dealing needed not to expend its efforts in the pursuit of forms. These were ready to be utilized by

The Netherland School

genius and perception. But, as it frequently happens with men of decided mental characteristics, Okeghem fell into excess of subtlety. It was reserved for his pupil, notably Josquin des Près, to mingle the scientific spirit with the melodious. This gifted man was for a period in Rome, and, indeed, it is the enthusiasm of the Netherland school that compels our admiration. They were not content to remain in the cities and land of their birth. They had a mission to fulfil, a new form of the beautiful to establish. They went with eager minds to work in general among eager peoples. Italians, Germans, and Spaniards benefited especially by the new mode of musical culture.

To mention a few of the greatest masters. Gombert laboured in Madrid, Arkadelt in Rome, Willaert in Venice; while Orlandus Lassus carried the perfection of his art to Munich. At Venice and Rome important schools were established by these apostles of the beautiful, and we in these later days reap the reward of their labours in oratorio, opera, and the drama.

Moreover, we incline to the belief that it was no casual impulse which compelled these earnest spirits of the North to mingle with the genius of the romantic South. For the delight, solace, and satisfaction of mankind in the exercise of one of the noblest of the arts, it was necessary that this fusion should take place, and to a philosophic mind, contemplating the various forces working in humanity, it affords yet another illustration of the evolution of the beautiful from diverse characteristics, ordained and perfected by the guiding spirit of all life.

THE PERIOD OF THE RENAISSANCE.

XIII.

THE RENAISSANCE.

THUS far in the history of music our reflections have been upon the conceptions, the initiatory efforts and attainments, of the ancient and early Christian world. For two thousand years, from the dawn of the exalted notions of the Chinese upon the harmonic utterance of the universe, to the wide and scientific achievements of the Netherland school, our thoughts have been impelled to follow the evolution of the tonal art. We have seen how religion, philosophy, and the other arts have affected her development; and now she is about to receive a new impulse, for humanity is in the birth-throes of the Renaissance, and the modern world is delivered at last.

The far-off ages gathered at her birth, and gave her offerings of the best. Plato bestowed the benediction of wisdom, Aristotle the gift of law; Virgil sang at her cradle, and the song sank with infinite sweetness into human hearts. Athens shook the wand of her enchantment over Florence, and the commingled intellect of Greek and Tuscan wrought in passionate exultation a dower of beauty for Earth's latest child. Its name is Liberty, and its nature is love; and, as if to symbolize the two, Columbus, by the gift of the spirit that was within him, flung back upon the floor of ocean the portals of another world, and Luther, by the Holy Spirit that compelled him, struck down the idol of a brazen Papacy, and gave men blessing for cursing.

The air was full of voices, the yearnings of humanity. Hell itself had given of its anguish, and heaven of its serenity, in Dante's immortal epics. Far away might be heard the lingering chorales of the monasteries, and nearer the denunciations of Savonarola. Michael Angelo saw visions of judgment, and Raphael idealized the conceptions of motherhood. The current of mental enthusiasm flowed over into different lands, quickening the forces of intellectual and spiritual life, breathing into learning and the arts the breath of humanity, and firing the mind of the age with the mingled heroism of genius and adventure.

And that art of all others best fitted to give utterance to the emotions generated by the Renaissance is music. Centuries of effort had at last endowed her with mastery over the laws wherein she could work in freedom, and when the heroic Luther stood out against the powers of the world to vindicate and uphold the rights of the individual conscience, Music brought the catholicity of her powers to the side of Liberty, and henceforth in hymns of winged gladness, in the passion of the drama, in the melody of opera, in the majesty of oratorio, she pours forth the emotions of the modern mind.

XIV.

THE INFLUENCE OF LUTHER.

I HAVE said that music brought the catholicity of her power to aid Luther in his heroic endeavour to free the consciences of men from the tyranny of Romish observance; but if this is so, it was because Luther, with the wisdom which is the corollary of true genius, wooed the noblest forms of the art to enter the service of the reformed religion.

A devoted lover and true critic of the spiritual and art mission of music, he saw clearly that there need be no divorce of the methods previously adopted. He was alone solicitous that these methods should be more freely used, and that the congregation should have liberal opportunities of expressing their emotion through the medium of song.

The cantus firmus, from which evolved the German chorale, was adopted by the Evangelical Church as a melody for the whole congregation; and in like manner portions of the Psalms, Gospels, lessons and collect tones, as well as antiphons, hymns, sequences, etc., were culled from the old Gregorian chorale.* But the great innovation of the Reformer was the introduction of the German congregational hymn—an innovation the importance of which it is difficult to estimate when considering the influence it subsequently exerted in the Protestant religious service.

Further, Luther brought home the liturgy to the people's understanding. He translated it almost entirely into German; but here, again, the congregational song was based on the form of the Roman Catholic chorale. The influence of Luther's genius in instituting and guiding these innovations in the musical service is seen in the marvellous growth of the art we are considering, for it speedily attained a freedom and spontaneity with which centuries of effort had failed to endow it under the more restricted methods of the Roman Catholic Church.

But while Luther, with rare penetration, selected freely from the art music of previous generations, so with equal penetration he discerned that the people's songs, the Volkslieder, were the media of their deepest emotions. These melodies were therefore introduced into the service, set to sacred instead of secular words.

Again, Luther's influence upon the development of music in Germany is discerned in his companionship with the most eminent of native musicians, notably with Henry Isaak and Ludwig

* Naumann, p. 428.

Senfel, whose culture was received from the Netherland school; but above all his esteem and admiration was reserved for Josquin des Près, of the school just mentioned, whose genius exercised so powerful an effect over contemporary German tone-masters.

It was while at the monastery of Erfurt that music took such firm possession of Luther, and there he perfected the musical education he had received when, as a lad, he had been chosen to take part in the congregational hymn and certain of the Church services. He especially devoted himself to contrapuntal studies, and that he had a wide and deep knowledge of polyphony is evidenced by the facility with which he detected the merits and defects of ambitious compositions, and with which he could re-write or improve certain of the melodies which he and others were accustomed to sing.

He likewise felt the importance of appropriate tones for the text, and laboured diligently in this direction when endeavouring to introduce the Mass written entirely in the German tongue for the benefit of his countrymen.

Modern criticism and controversy render it difficult to decide whether Luther can be regarded as an original composer; but be this as it may, his genius was the great native force which moulded the future of Protestant musical service, and this, surely, is sufficient encomium for one man.

Luther's home-life would appear to have been very charming. After the labours of the day he would gather around him those he loved, and surrender himself freely to the enjoyment of musical compositions. Among his friends might be seen Melancthon and Walther, the last-named of whom was bound to him by a pure affection, as purely reciprocated. Indeed, Walther was Luther's great co-worker in bringing home to the hearts of the people the mission of music, and likewise as the composer of several beautiful and pathetic melodies. Walther's great talent lay in melodic composition, and it was he who published the Wittenberg sacred song-book.

XV.

VENICE AND ADRIAN WILLAERT.

WE have previously remarked upon the enthusiasm exhibited by the Netherland tone-masters, and their exalted endeavours in the cause of art. We have now to consider more fully the effect of their genius as shown in the formation of the various Italian schools.

It might superficially appear to be an anomaly that a people so gifted as the Italians in the fifteenth century, so keenly sensitive to the intellectual and the beautiful, should have been indebted to men whose imaginations could never have received such mental wave-shocks of culture as those resident in a land which first felt, and was first capable of receiving, the flood of long pent-up knowledge of the classic eras—a knowledge so calculated to arouse enthusiasm, and to kindle into full activity the mental faculties.

But although we must not forget that the Netherlands was a home of song, and that powerful guilds of musicians had been established therein, yet the explanation of this enigma, if one be wanting, lay in the fact that the Renaissance appealed rather to the intellectual than to the spiritual faculties of the Italians, whereas the Netherlander, deep, earnest, and broadly human, was religious and reflective. If this be so, then in the pure domain of art a fusion of the characteristics of both peoples could but result in progress and in new and varied combinations.

Thus, in the great law of mental economy, which no less governs the genius of peoples than of individuals, the several intellectual and spiritual qualities react upon each other, generating arts and sciences, the outcome of commingled ideas, different times and altered circumstances. Let us, then, trace the influence of the Netherlander and Italian in the development of music, and study it first in the rise of the Venetian school.

The master to whom belongs the honour of initiating harmonic combinations, as understood to-day, is Adrian Willaert, and the city honoured by his labours was Venice, a city which, as the master first beheld it in 1526, was not perceptibly shorn of its glory, although it had suffered in its honour, and was destined to pathetic decay and bitter humiliation. We know not whether Willaert was aware of its momentous history—a history which, in its earlier part, is illumined for centuries with the light of religious devotion and the virtues of constancy and fortitude. Neither do we know whether he was acquainted with the far less honourable incidents of its later career, or with the wonderful influences which had produced the art life of the brilliant city.

Be this as it may, it was particularly appropriate that modern harmony should here have its birth—here, too, in the Church of St. Mark, for to this sanctuary likewise the Arab and Lombard, the East and the West, had brought their united gifts of intellect and spirit, and had woven them into fairest vesture of harmonious colouring, as if preparing to clothe the child new-born. Yes, truly so; for St. Mark's contained a double organ, which suggested to Willaert the notion of double choruses, the compositions for which he based upon harmonic structure according to our modern notions.

Thus, then, at Venice man, through the gift of the Spirit of God, harmonized the elements into a dwelling-place for Christ's Bride. The Lombard and Arab harmonized the rugged human energy and passion of the North with the rapt devotional contemplation of the East, so that architecture reflected both form and spirit; the brothers Bellini founded a new school of harmonious colouring; and Willaert harmonized the melodies and aspirations of man's emotions.

The master of whom we are speaking instinctively felt the necessity of making the various parts of his double choruses administer a mutual support to the design and the effect of the composition as a whole. The melodies were no longer independent, but subservient to the ultimate purpose and character of the work, being woven into each other, according to the modern law of contrapuntal working. The gain to the art was incalculable, and here, at last, the striving of the centuries and the efforts for attainment of numerously gifted minds found realization of their desire.

The correct methods of polyphony established by Willaert were speedily utilized by his pupils and successors. The imperious necessity of colour induced Cyprian de Rore to a frequent use of chromatic intervals, whereby emotion could be more freely and truthfully expressed; while the gifted Gabrielis, uncle and nephew, still further provided for this necessity by the blending of voices and instruments in the symphoniæ sacræ. This latter innovation was a great gain to the art, for from it ultimately issued a free and independent existence for instrumental music.

XVI.

ROME AND PALESTRINA.

FROM the beauty and repose of Venice we pass to the grandeur of Rome. A long line of distinguished masters, Dufay, Josquin des Près, Arkadelt, Goudimel, and others, had established therein the methods and principles of the Netherland school, and each had in his direction contributed to the emancipation of music from conventionality. Men of undoubted attainment, imbued with the majesty of their art, they prepared the way for the noble and gifted Palestrina, who by his serene genius and sympathy exalted polyphony to as lofty and secure an eminence as the allied arts of painting and architecture had been raised to by Raphael and Michael Angelo.

The particular characteristics of Italian genius most happily supplemented those of the Netherland masters, bringing to earnestness and science a quick perception of the needs which music suffered, and interweaving with profound knowledge the qualities of simpleness and grace. (Goudimel, the direct master of Palestrina, who had gathered round him at Rome a number of gifted pupils, displays in his compositions a marked advance towards melodic utterance, but much remained to be accomplished in this direction.

But a few years previously there had passed away from Rome a genius who had raised the art of painting to unequalled and never-to-be-surpassed perfection. By the qualities of grace, tenderness and majesty, Raphael summed up in his Madonnas and religious compositions the abiding, lovable, and inspiring characteristics of Roman Catholicism, rendering in the language of his art the worthiest tribute to God and womanhood which has yet been expressed by mortal man. And as he exhausted the knowledge of his time, veiling under the simplicity of his style all that Italy could teach, so Palestrina, throughout his career, stage by stage, evolved from the contrapuntal knowledge which he inherited the enduring qualities of melodic grace and simple grandeur which exalted polyphony to a sublime and most spiritualized expression. But not at once did Palestrina arrive at freedom under the bonds of law. The first volume of his publications abounds in the methods and intricacies of the Netherland school; in the second his genius has gained partial freedom; in the third it has conquered, leading science captive with melodic grace and charm.

We need not follow in detail the incidents of Palestrina's somewhat chequered career. Although compelled by Paul IV. to leave the body of collegiate singers through certain disqualifications, yet his genius won such renown in the 'Crux Fidelis,' and a collection of Improparia, written in 1560 for eight voices, that the Pope begged they might be performed in the Vatican. Quickly following on his expulsion, Palestrina was appointed Maestro della Cappella at the Lateran, and well-nigh immediately afterwards transferred to a similar position at Santa Maria Maggiore.

In 1571 he was again Maestro at the Vatican, and it was during the period between 1561 and 1571 that his genius ripened, and his style assumed those special characteristics upon which was based the future music of the Catholic Church. And, indeed, the Church music of Palestrina's day required reform, for such was the laxity of its performance that the Council of Trent condemned it in unmeasured terms.

The outcome of the Council's admonition was the appointment, in 1563, of a commission of eight Cardinals to inquire into the condition of the musical service, and to report thereon to the Pope. Palestrina was invited to furnish a Mass as a type of sacred music, and in compliance submitted three, one of which was the famed 'Missa Papæ Marcelli.' This Mass was performed before the commission on April 28, 1565, and met with unequalled success. By it the future of Church music was determined.

The genius of the Præneste master had extracted from the works of his predecessors their valuable qualities, and, discarding contrapuntal excesses, substituted a direct and simple utterance clothed with the beauty and grace of melody. Many years of honoured labour lay before him after his reappointment to the Vatican in 1571, years in which he established a school in conjunction with his friend Giovanni Maria Nanini. His influence was thus preserved, and largely affected the future of European music.

It is difficult to aptly express in a few words what we feel concerning the style of this master, but it is so important to arrive at a clear conception of its characteristics that we determine, at the risk of repetition, briefly to summarize them. Thus, Palestrina simplified the law of contrapuntal working, not, indeed, discarding the labours of his predecessors, but honouring them by basing his work upon their methods. The majesty of their compositions he doubtless felt, and the truthfulness of their art forms; but, seeing they had been led into an excess of subtle and perplexing intricacies, he confined himself to a simple and direct utterance, leaving to his æsthetic instincts the management of the various voices, while his genius supplied from the fountain of its inspiration that spiritual emotion, that flow of grace and melody, which, in the art of pure polyphony, have never been more abundantly poured forth.

XVII.

ROME AND ORATORIO.

THE mantle of Palestrina fell upon Gregorio Allegri, a distinguished and worthy successor; but Rome was to receive yet further honour through Giacomo Carissimi (1604-1674), whose genius evolved from the sacred cantata the art form known as oratorio. This form was the ultimate result of two great influences—the one a keen desire throughout the Middle Ages to attain some adequate mode of expression to provide for the feelings called forth by the perusal of the sacred narrative; the other the study of the Greek drama throughout Italy, and the consideration of the part which music played therein. This consideration gave rise to the monodic form, a melody written with a distinctive purpose for one voice. In polyphony there was no such distinctive melody, but in the oratorio—the noblest form of which music is capable to express by solo and chorus the intense feeling of the individual, and the majesty of enlarged and general emotion—the influences we have mentioned created a channel for dramatic utterance, along which the current of Carissimi's genius freely flowed.

In Florence the cultivation of the monodic form, with other influences which we shall presently consider, gave birth to opera, whereas the issue in Rome was oratorio. The two forms are the result of mental and spiritual law in art. Opera was the child of cultured and intellectual Florence, oratorio the offspring of emotional and religious Rome.

In the Middle Ages a necessity for dramatic appeal to the feelings of the people is evinced by the mystery, morality, and miracle plays so prevalent and esteemed throughout Europe. We can well imagine how pathetic and stirring to simple souls must have been the visible realization of our Lord's Passion, but naturally it was in Rome that this exhibition would be peculiarly appropriate.

In such exhibitions the germ of oratorio lay hidden, and we find the name first applied to a series of performances given by Filippo Neri in the oratory of the Church of Santa Maria Vallicella. Following Filippo Neri came Emilio del Cavaliere. In common with his contemporaries, he endeavoured to find an appropriate musical setting for dramatic utterance, and a sacred play, written for him by Laura Guidiccioni, entitled ' La Rappresentazione dell' Anima e del Corpo,' was produced in the month of February, 1600, at the Church of Santa Maria Vallicella, ten months before Peri's 'Eurydice' at Florence. Succeeding Cavaliere we find Kapsberger, Vittorio Loreto, and Michel Angelo Rossi, until Domenico Mazzochi heralded by his enthusiastic cultivation of the monodic style, and his earnest endeavours to make it a worthy vehicle of musical and dramatic expression, the genius of Giacomo Carissimi.

Before Carissimi the majority of writers had failed to understand that in the fusion of music and rhetoric the latter could only attain its noblest influence when allied with appropriate music. In the two arts thus combined, neither could be independent of the other. The various feelings of which the text was the theme received an interpretation of truthfulness and value impossible to overestimate when the tonal art brought its prolific resources of expression to illustrate the universality of the soul's emotion. Only one art can adequately express the most subtle shades of human feeling, and verbal utterance, however inspired, can never sound the depths of these emotions without the combined aid of music. Carissimi perceived this as no other writer in the realm of sacred feeling had done before him. Hence he always strove that the music should worthily interpret the text, and perceiving that his art ever occupied the noblest position as the source of religious feeling, he brought his genius to fructify and quicken the labours of the monodist, and by his imagination, sympathy, and spiritual insight, allied with adequate technical knowledge, he wrought into the glorious form of oratorio the yearning efforts of his day after worthy expression of dramatic feeling in the breadth, depth, and sublimity of religious devotion.

XVIII.

OPERA.

IN our later considerations the realm of musical feeling has greatly widened. Willaert, Palestrina, Carissimi, have wrought therein as master workers, and the sense of immaturity has faded. In all her newly acquired majesty, in all the breadth and grandeur of her spiritual freedom, noble, serene, conscious of development in beauty and power, the art of music arises in abstract loveliness upon the mental vision. To the soul capable of perception, harmony and virtue are embodied in forms replete with beauty ineffable, filled with the arts of healing and consolation, yet creating deep spiritual unrest, the desire of the soul to be with its beloved, the condition precedent to all nobler being.

Venice and Rome, with their associations, detain us at present no longer. We pass to a city, like to none other, by the side of Arno, and Florence and the memories that passionately cleave to her arise before us. What other city of the modern world so fascinates the attention? What other city in equal measure with the brief period of her greatness bred and inspired such sons of genius? What other city was so passionately beloved of her citizens, save Athens and Jerusalem of old? Yea, even Athens, in the resurrection of her genius, appeared first to Florence, as if there was some subtle feeling in the breast of Time that she was her worthiest successor. What drama of passion and hatred, what dreams of sweetness and love, unfold within her history! what joy and lamentation echo from her walls!

A city adorned with beauty, nestling amidst her olive groves, with the encircling hills around her, down whose gentle slopes in the forefront of the year the spring came sweetly stealing to greet the Florentines with the kiss of mirthful love, to fill their hearts with gladness, and to crown their children with the garlands of innocence and hope. How could gloom linger in such a joy-impelling season? By the side of Arno the citizens assembled, giving themselves to rejoicing, and poetry came with the gift of expression, and music with the heart's full feeling. Thus, from earliest times were slowly preparing those dramatic forces which, in conjunction with others, culminated in opera.

As environment in Venice and Rome greatly affected the form of art, so here in Florence we observe the same working of natural law. The desire which knew no rest until it had evolved a form of art capable of illustrating the light and shadow of human life was but a natural heritage of that past, so glorious and inquisitive, so gentle yet aspiring, so prophetic and religious, so intellectually titanic, which is the strength and pride of the Tuscan city.

Where could opera be born but here? Here, where Dante mused in the first glory of his manhood, every conception purified by the ennobling passion of that love whose sweetness, sorrow, and despair has touched and quickened the human heart, laying bare the depths of hell and unveiling the serenity of heaven. Here, too, where Cimabue, with Giotto, from the mountain-side, fresh from the folding of his sheep, wrought undying victory in art; where Boccaccio, Petrarch, Brunelleschi, and Donatello gave each his meed; where Fra Angelico disclosed to mortals his angelic visions, and Lorenzo, the gifted and the dissolute, held sway. Here, too, where Machiavelli, prince of cynicism, mingled side by side with Savonarola, prophet and martyr, and where Michael Angelo laboured and triumphed, grieving for his country even with bitter tears.

In such a society were all mental elements, and add to these the Greek spirit, mingling with the Tuscan intellect, and those ferocious party passions which knew no cessation within or without the walls of Florence, and we have the emotions which opera portrays. The stranger did not mould Florence, but Florence moulded the stranger. Hence, we find that those Netherlanders, Hobrect, Josquin des Près, Agricola, and Isaak, failed to found a school of sacred music. The influence of Hellenism was too paramount. The tragedies of Æschylus and Sophocles, rather than Isaiah and the Gospels, were the favourite reading of those Florentines run riot with the new wine of Greek learning.

In such a city cultured dilettanti naturally abounded—men impatient of tradition, seeking to find some form wherein to embody the restless cravings of their nature for the beautiful. They turned to those tragedies we have mentioned, endeavouring to convey their sense to the people by scenic effect and appropriate music. In this they failed, yet signal honour befell them; indeed, it was not likely they could revive those immortal works as originally presented. Once only in all time has been bestowed upon man that perfect balance of genius and temperament, that serene power and calm, which wrought perfection in this sphere of art. It was not that the Florentines were incapable of appreciating dramatic productions. Had they been so, opera would have been born elsewhere. So far back as the fourteenth century dramatic representations in the festivals of the city were familiar to the people, and these plays were interspersed by music written by the ablest composers of the day. Hence, their musical compositions were called intermezzi. These intermezzi seem to have consisted of madrigals sung by the chorus, the text always having some relation to the action of the play, and this primitive conception of song and drama continued to the latter part of the sixteenth century.

For the text, intended for an individual rendering, to be sung by a five-part chorus in the form of a madrigal, was indeed unsatisfactory. The occasion of the marriage of Bianca Capello with Francesco, Duke of Tuscany, brought this dissatisfaction to a crisis, by a violent outburst of feeling, on the part of the Florentine nobility, against the Venetian composers, Claudio Merullo and Andrea Gabrieli. These masters had composed the festal music, according to the prevailing methods of polyphony and strict laws of canon.

A meeting of the dilettanti, with Count Bardi at their head, determined, if possible, to discover some method of accompanying the drama with appropriate music. Associated with Bardi in this enterprise were Corsi, Ottavio Rinuccini, Pietro Strozzi, Emilio del Cavaliere, and last, but not least, Vincenzo Galilei, the celebrated father of a more celebrated son. This band waged incessant war against the school of contrapuntists, and indicated the new method to be pursued by composing a dramatic scena for one voice with the accompaniment of a single instrument.

The merit of this innovation belongs to Galilei. The subjects were 'Ugolino,' from Dante's 'Purgatorio,' and the 'Lamentations of Jeremiah.'

These efforts met with deserved success, and thus was established the monody, the essential element for the further development of dramatic music. Following Galilei were Giulio Caccini and Emilio del Cavaliere, and then arose in the firmament of art Jacope Peri. It was owing to the reflective genius of this master that the efforts of the dilettanti were productive of such rich result. He entered deeply into the spirit of the Greek drama, and, assuming that in its original presentation it received expression rather by tonal colouring than actual song, he set himself to study the various modes of speech in daily life, from which he evolved the form of musical setting employed in his operas of 'Daphne' and 'Eurydice.' To quote a passage from Naumann on this subject:

'Soft and gentle speech he interpreted by half-spoken, half-sung tones on a sustained instrumental bass; feelings of a deeper emotional kind by a melody with greater intervals and a lively tempo, the accompanying instrumental harmonies changing more frequently. Sometimes he employed dissonances. This was the beginning of the dramatic recitative, and the honour of its invention is Peri's.'

The deserved success which followed the representation of these two operas naturally gave a great stimulus to dramatic music throughout Italy. Florence, Mantua, Bologna, Venice, were especially distinguished, and Monteverde, inspired by Peri, became the most accomplished dramatic composer of the seventeenth century.

The genius of Monteverde ill accorded with the theoretical teachings of his day. Like all men of genius, it was necessary that he should follow his natural inclinations. The Tuscan drama had, indeed, kindled that genius, but it had likewise called into being a craving which the monodic form was unable to appease. Whoever has listened to the modern orchestra, of which Monteverde was the founder, will understand that the various phases of emotion cannot with sufficiency be interpreted by the voice. Monody, indeed, was essential in the evolution of musical drama; but the instinct which established it was but half fulfilled without the full resources of instrumental art which are embodied in the orchestra.

Dissatisfaction, the supreme gift of the true artist, leading to new discoveries and endeavours in the attainment of the ideal, impelled Monteverde to seek in the orchestra the means of producing that tonal colouring which the voice is unable adequately to express. His sympathetic instincts led him at once to a true reform upon the method of his predecessors. He relied for the attainment of this desire upon stringed instruments played with the bow, and thus secured for himself and others that wonderful instrument, the orchestra, which translates the emotions of the soul into perfect utterance.

His writing for the violin called into existence a class of virtuosi, of whom Corelli may be named as a brilliant example, and inspired the successful efforts of the Amatis, Stradivari and Guarneri, to provide an instrument which would enable the performer to work thereon his own will.

That Monteverde was fruitful in resource may be evidenced by his invention of the tremolo and pizzicato, and, indeed, in this master we see a kindred genius with that of the maestro Richard Wagner, whose soul sought in Nature direct inspiration. With these remarks we take leave of Monteverde before we return hurriedly to Venice, and thence pass by way of Naples to the establishment of opera proper upon the soil of France.

XIX.

LOTTI AND FRESCOBALDI.

WE left Venice at the moment when the Gabrielis had introduced into their Church compositions orchestral effects. Under these masters music had indeed advanced a stage onward in the course of her development; but still the advance was founded on Netherland influence. The interval of fifty years which had elapsed between the Gabrielis, the representatives of the old Venetian school, and the representatives of the new Venetian school in the persons of Legrenzi, Lotti and Caldara, were years which felt the powerful influence of the Reformation and the onflowing tide of the Renaissance.

The purer spirit which manifested itself in music under the guiding genius of Luther was not without its effect upon the Catholic works of this new Venetian school. They saw it was essential, in the interests of their religion, that music should appeal as powerfully as in the Protestant service to the spiritual and emotional faculties. Hence they imparted to their art increased animation, combined with grandeur and pathetic earnestness. These remarks specially apply to Lotti, the pupil of Legrenzi. He felt the sacredness of his art, and endeavoured in his treatment to clothe it with a noble and spiritualized expression.

Before again taking leave of Venice, we would remark upon the influence it exerted throughout Lombardy and the North of Italy generally. This influence was powerfully felt amongst the members of the renowned school of Italian organists, of whom Girolamo Frescobaldi was the chief. A master of the old Church modes and of the modern system of scales, he likewise revived the double counterpoint of the old French school. His compositions, especially his employment of the instrumental fugue, prepared the way for Lotti and Scarlatti, Bach and Handel. Indeed, instrumental music generally throughout the North of Italy at this period strove in emotional intensity, elaboration and reproduction of the same subject under various conceptions, to embody the influence which the Renaissance wrought in mental and moral life, thus keeping alive that spirit of the ideal which the Germans sought and wooed so successfully in the coming generations.

XX.

NAPLES AND SCARLATTI.

WE now pass to the consideration of the third great school of music established on Italian soil, a school which, even as those established in Venice and Rome, reflects the peculiar conditions of its environment. The genius of Italy, though destined to act powerfully for all time upon the thought of Europe, and to spread in ever-widening circles, was peculiarly under the sway of local feelings and conditions. How truly, for instance, were Dante and Michael Angelo sons of Florence, and Palestrina a son of Rome!

And now at Naples a genius was to arise in Alessandro Scarlatti to reflect her influence in the tonal art, and to throw the glamour of her beauty for a century athwart the purer spiritual vision of the North. Yes, Naples was indeed lovely—a loveliness which had attracted in the centuries long gone the pleasure-loving Greek and luxurious Roman. But it is often thus. In earth's fairest places the spirit of earth prevails. The mind, blinded by the veil of temporal beauty, sees not into those regions beyond, where every effort is purified, and the soul seeks to ally itself with the absolutely perfect.

The spirit of harmony might indeed have felt, as she winged her flight from the city on the Tiber, where dwelt in the memories of men faded but never-to-be-obliterated greatness, and where for centuries earth's purest children had come for worship and repose, howsoever now fallen from imperial majesty and true saintliness, that in this her new abode of Naples, where the sunlight kissed the sea into murmuring ecstasy of song, that here, at least, in reflections upon surpassing beauty, new revelations would be made to her, and that her voice, uprising in ever-increasing power and sweetness unsurpassed of song, should be indeed a solace for the whole earth. But the time was not yet. Naples attached herself to melody, the reflex of the ease, grace, and fertility with which she was enveloped giving powerful stimulus to certain forms of the art; but after Scarlatti not one of her children was able to continue and perfect in adequate measure the principles established by him.

Scarlatti, like his gifted predecessor, Stradella, was a pupil of Carissimi, and he early felt the powerful influence of the Tuscan drama. Perfectly familiar with the scientific methods of the

Netherlander, and assimilating the true art elements of monody, music-drama, and the oratorio, he softened by beauteous melody the forms bequeathed by Netherlander and Tuscan. His compositions for the Church gave rise to a new style—a style in which he substituted for the old thematic counterpoint a freer development of parts, which soon gained the favour of musicians and people.

The efforts of the Tuscans to discover and supply the Greek renderings of the drama were necessarily futile. The modern spirit could only effectually work in its own way. The calm dignity, grace, and perfect proportions which are so conspicuously manifest in the best period of Greek art were doubtless equally manifest in the production of the drama, and how beautiful and appropriate the rendering we now can only imagine.

But the mental and spiritual characteristics of the seventeenth century were widely sundered from those of the fourth century before Christ, and Scarlatti concerned himself not with vain efforts to resuscitate a form of genius the outcome of the peculiar characteristics of its own age, but to adapt what the ages had bequeathed to modern conditions. And the prevalent modern condition was emotion and passionate unrest, rather than intellectual and æsthetic balance. The modern world, however influenced by Attic genius, could never be Grecian in its deepest sympathies. Christianity had imported a new element into life, a new ideal, and that of the soul rather than of the mind. Scarlatti therefore severed himself from Tuscan methods. He, indeed, took the monody, but changed it from its declamatory to a melodic character, elevating it to dominion over poetry, instead of keeping it, as hitherto, subject to her authority. Melody was the goal of Scarlatti's efforts, the central force of the school he founded; but the peculiar danger to which melody is subject soon became apparent, and when Scarlatti's guiding genius was withdrawn, melody, unsupported by polyphonic structure, inevitably declined into untruthful, formal, and sensual exhibition, while the rise of the mere virtuosi, with their claims, jealousies, and bickerings, portended but disaster for the coming days.

To Scarlatti, then, modern music is greatly indebted for the characteristics of grace, charm, and flexibility. The Neapolitan school was the disseminator of opera, and influenced considerably other Italian schools, such as the musico-dramatic schools of Venice, Rome, Milan; and Italian methods and Italian virtuosi flooded the Continent of Europe. Everything in music, as in the other arts, was subject to the teaching of the Italians. In Germany their influence was most baneful, and they seldom knew, or, knowing, appreciated, these prophets which arose in that nation, who by the glorious majesty and truthfulness of their utterance were ultimately to arrest the temporary decline of music, and to carry it in many of its branches to the summit of its attainment and perfection.

XXI.

FRENCH OPERA.

ITALY has long detained us by her genius—by those mental characteristics which fitted her so pre-eminently to initiate a new order in art. But we must now leave the narrative of her achievement to consider the art as exhibited in France, which country had long since surrendered her supremacy in this connection. Our consideration, however, will only concern that form selected as the subject of this chapter, namely, opera.

The seventeenth century found France, indeed, imbued with the idea of opera, an idea fostered and encouraged by her intercourse with Italy. The Tuscan music drama was directly imported into Paris under the patronage of Mazarin, and Peri's 'Eurydice' met with sympathetic reception. That such reception would be sympathetic was wellnigh certain under the circumstances, for the drama was being welded into a great national institution at this period by Corneille, Racine, Molière, and lesser ights. Therefore it was inevitable that a powerful stimulus would be applied to an art so appealing to French characteristics and sentiment as opera. Such stimulus was applied mainly by two men, Giovanni Battista Lully and Jean Philippe Rameau—the former a son of Italy, the latter of France.

Lully, born 1633, at or near Florence, early showed great aptitude for music. Attracting the notice of the Chevalier de Guise, he was taken by that nobleman to Paris, and entered into the service of Mademoiselle Montpensier. Here he perfected himself upon the guitar and violin, but, satirizing his mistress, was dismissed. He clung to his art, however, taking lessons in composition and organ-playing, and, still a mere youth, entered the service of Louis XIV. as violinist. His powers must have rapidly developed, for he soon became director of the orchestra known as Les Violons du Roy. After several essays in minor compositions he collaborated with Molière, writing the music to 'La Princesse d'Elide' and 'L'Amour Médecin.' Through circumstances which we need not mention, he obtained the patent for operatic representation in Paris, and thereafter directed his great gifts to the perfecting of French opera. Of those gifts, the most important, perhaps, was dramatic instinct, keen sensibility to appropriate representation. With the sympathy of genius, he passed easily from grave to gay, from the heroic to the comic, exhibiting in all styles power and confidence. Consistency and the gift of proportion in Lully foiled the evil tendency manifested by the Neapolitan school to elaborate and elevate the solo unduly for mere display of virtuosity. He employed his chorus, too, far more fully and effectively in the working of the drama than his Italian compatriots, and supported the recitative with orchestral accompaniment. His sensibility to effect led him, as might be supposed, to study the peculiar qualities of the several instruments, whether employed singly or in combination. In fact, conscientiousness, a minute study of details, was one of Lully's strong characteristics, and neither librettist nor musician escaped rigorous supervision. The valuable qualities of French declamation, neatness, aptitude, conciseness, combined with that formal conception of the drama supposed to be after classic models, found reflection in Lully's work. He was possessed peculiarly of those gifts necessary to enable him to establish on a firm basis in opera the style and characteristics which at this period moulded the French drama. Of commanding intellect and subtlety of resource, he met as equals the great writers of the day.

The same impulse and necessity which established French drama established French opera: one was corollary to the other. Of course perfection must not be looked for in Lully's work. The solo as solo fell below the Neapolitan standard. The ensemble also was weaker, as also the polyphonic structure. His harmony is sometimes defective, and his arias are usually fashioned after Corelli, Peri and Carissimi. The same rhythm and counterpoint are employed to illustrate different phases both of emotion and action, but notwithstanding he performed a great work which stamps him as a man of pre-eminent powers and ability.

The immediate followers of Lully added but little in originality or method to the form which he established. It was reserved to the musician already named, Jean Philippe Rameau, born at Dijon in 1683, to complete the work commenced so successfully by the Italian master. Rameau was eminently French in his mental characteristics, and although his powers were long in arriving at maturity, yet, having reached that point, they were ceaseless in activity. Like Lully, the love of music was manifested early, and after a few boyish escapades he was sent as a youth to study in Italy. Unfortunately for his after-labours, he eschewed the study of Italian methods, and quickly enrolled himself as a member of a travelling troupe of musicians. The joys of this existence having faded, he devoted himself whilst at Montpellier, whither he had come, to serious study, and, resolving to carve out a career, found his way to Paris in 1717. The jealousy of Louis Marchand, however, after he had extended his patronage to the unknown artist for a brief period, induced him to leave for Lille, from whence he went to

Clermont, occupying there, as at Lille, the position of organist. Here his previous studies of the works of Descartes, Mersenne, and Zarlino came, tendered by reflection, to richest result, issuing in the celebrated treatise, 'Traité d'Harmonie,' published subsequently at Paris in 1722. In this treatise he demonstrated that the system of harmony then prevailing was based on scientific or natural principles, and by it laid the foundation for a philosophic science of the art he had considered. Another celebrated work, 'Nouveau Système de Musique Théorique,' was published in 1726, also at Paris, whither he had returned in 1721.

Rameau's ambition, if in part consoled by his success in the domain of theory, was, however, still without satisfaction in operatic writing. His resolute genius, fortified by scientific study, was now impatient to earn those legitimate triumphs felt to be so securely within its power, but these triumphs were unattainable until a libretto was forthcoming which would satisfy the critical demands of the Académie. In vain did Rameau apply to Houdar de Lamotte for a lyric tragedy, assuring him of his capacities as a musician. At last fortune seemingly relented. Through the agency of his patron Popelinière he obtained from Voltaire the libretto of 'Samson,' but, the music completed, the Académie refused performance on account of the nature of the subject. At length the Abbé Pellegrin supplied him with the opera

'Hippolyte et Aricie,' in five acts, which was duly performed in 1733. Its presentation was the signal for a prolonged and bitter contest between the disciples of Lully and those of Rameau. Rameau's genius, however, could not be denied. In fruitful activity opera after opera was produced, winning their way to favour through stern opposition and acrimonious criticism. What, then, were these qualities which aroused such antipathy to the work of Rameau, based as it was in general upon that of Lully?

Rameau's great characteristic was innovation. True genius never consents to follow abjectly previous methods. Lully's followers adhered strictly to the forms bequeathed by him, but Rameau from the first introduced variations, and substituting 'new forms, varied and piquant rhythms, ingenious harmonies, bold modulations, and a richer and more effective orchestration,' he claimed and retained the attention of his hearers. He also endeavoured, and with success, to give a distinct part to each instrument, and to introduce his operas with a well-constructed overture, nor did he neglect to develop the chorus, while the rhythm and melody of his ballet music was so pleasing that it was speedily adopted and copied in the theatres of Italy and Germany.*

* See article 'Rameau': Grove's 'Dictionary of Musicians.'

XXII.

THE PRECURSORS OF THE GREAT TONE POETS.

HAVING briefly examined the rise of opera in France, we turn to Germany, which detained us last when considering the influence which the vigorous genius of Luther had upon the music of the period. We have already seen how salutary that influence was, how it brought home to the hearts of the people a pure and strong tonality; and doubtless it laid the foundation for a period yet far subsequent, when the German nation should occupy the foremost position in the most universal of the arts.

In mental qualities the Netherlander and German are allied. In both serious reflection and a deep religious basis set them pondering upon the mysteries of life. Tone as tone, the desire in the art for mere recreation or for refined enjoyment, could not satisfy minds so vigorous and analytical, yet so filled with humility in resting in and searching after the deep things of God. True, for some time the German mind did not arrive at that clear consciousness of itself, that powerful individuality, bold and uncompromising, which yet was to assimilate the complex forms of art, and to reissue them blent with awakened life and thought in glorious epic or masterly portrayal of emotion charged with lyric sweetness.

Such pre-eminence was the work of centuries, centuries of communing and selection, of long years of passive reception of foreign influences, of silent growth and assimilation before the moment came for deliverance and freedom under the laws of art. Of foreign influences the Italian was naturally very powerful. The German mind was thirsting for beauty, and Italy was the fountain whence flowed the streams of culture. German masters made pilgrimages to Venice or to Rome, studying there the methods of the Gabrielis, of Frescobaldi and Carissimi, and upon their return endeavoured to introduce the various excellences and styles they had attained to their fellow-countrymen.

Among such men were Kerl and Froberger. Both were renowned organists, the latter, in his contrapuntal and fugal compositions, having a considerable influence over Sebastian Bach. For the fugal form Germany was specially indebted to Italy. It was reserved for the great master Bach not to originate the form, as has been popularly supposed, but to use it as the chief interpreter of his wonderful genius and deep religious feeling.

Muffat and Biber, who in part received their education from Italy, devoted their talents to the cause of instrumentation, seeking to imbue their countrymen with higher artistic feeling both in composition and technique. Their labours came at an opportune moment, for Germany was then turning her attention to the improvement of the solo instruments. But mingling with this direct current of Italian influence was yet another—the influence of the Netherlander.

Swelinck, the great organist of this latter school, had indeed, a century and a half anterior to Bach, drunk deeply of Venetian inspiration, and, returning to Amsterdam, founded a school, the fame of whose pupils will never die. Scheidt, Scheidemann and Schultz are the most renowned, but above these are the names of Reinken and Buxtehude, whose influence over Bach was direct and paramount. Reinken was a pupil of Scheidemann, while Buxtehude was instructed by his father, probably in the traditions of the Swelinck school. To both these masters Bach made pilgrimages of love. Twice he visited Reinken at Hamburg, and on the latter occasion, when extemporizing before this master, received from his lips these memorable words:

'I thought this art had died out, but I see that it lives in you.'

That Buxtehude should possess a great attraction for Bach we can well understand. Buxtehude's brilliant gifts, both of composition and of playing, his noble enthusiasm for the art, the heroic nature of his labours in connection with those memorable sacred concerts held on Sunday evenings at St. Mary's Church at Lübeck, all would claim admiration from an artist of Bach's earnest temperament; and, indeed, in Bach's organ compositions is to be traced the abiding influence of this master. But mingling with the labours of Swelinck's disciples were those of the masters of Mid-Germany, who inherited the Lutheran traditions in congregational song.

The names of Franck, Johann Hermann Schein, Andreas Hammerschmidt, the two uncles of Sebastian Bach, Johann Christopher and Johann Michael, with that of Johann Pachelbel, are those of the prominent masters of this group. Their great work was the perfection of choral song. Our brief remarks show how earnestly in the seventeenth century Germany was endeavouring to find utterance in music; but there are yet three names of special import: Michael Prætorius, Heinrich Schütz, and Johann Joseph Fux.

Each of these three men was endowed with a thorough knowledge of Italian and German forms. In their enthusiasm for Italy, they laboured to introduce all that was noteworthy and excellent. The greater dramatic instinct, the richer tone, colouring, and graceful melodic treatment, all found, and that rightly, admiration and emulation in these masters; but at the same time patriotism and sacred regard for national thought and feeling ever forbade them to be merely followers instead of mediators. They, too, had a message to

Precursors of the Great Tone Poets 109

deliver and a mission to accomplish, even as the great masters of Italy. The awakening thought of Germany, its steadfast faith and satisfaction in religion, were equally with the Italian qualities mentioned woven into their compositions, thus establishing a sure foundation for those majestic tonal epics to be subsequently produced.

Perhaps enough has been said to show what various influences were preparing the way for the ascendency of Germany in the tonal art. True, for a time the latter-day principles of the Neapolitan school, pernicious and rhetorical, strove to contaminate the purity and majesty of conception which eventually led the noblest minds of Germany to prepare an everlasting solace and delight of song for the Western mind; but before turning our attention to those blest poets, whose inspiration fed by virtue, and whose loving spirits caught from far the beauteous accents of celestial song, we will briefly endeavour to realize what were the conditions of life around them, so as to be better prepared to estimate the principles which guided them in the production of their immortal compositions.

In speaking of the Neapolitan school, after paying a tribute to the genius of Scarlatti, we had to confess that it was greatly responsible for the departure from those true methods of composition which had been pursued so faithfully by the master spirits whose labours we have considered. The decline, not only in the tonal art, but in the other arts, may be referred to a temporary exhaustion of that marvellous energy which had been remoulding European thought and society during the fifteenth, sixteenth, and seventeenth centuries. Such a wonderful vista had been opened to the human understanding, so many constituent elements of emotion had been discovered, as it were, in man's organization. The currents that thrilled him had been continuous and powerful. The opening of new worlds in the domain of thought, the reconstitution and defence of religion, the dawn of modern art arising to meridional splendour, and the dim conceptions of great social changes, the murmuring of the nations awaiting a diviner method whose monotones sounded afar off, mysterious and awe-inspiring, would seem to have weaned human energy.

The great ideals before the minds of men, which in art were to issue in the noblest forms of music, and in a profound literature, philosophic, analytical, and creative, no longer in the eighteenth century lay in dazzling brilliance before the European mind. Italy had fallen from her high estate. The great intellects and master spirits which had raised her to such pre-eminence found no capable successors. They who came after knew not that wrestling, that conflict, out of which had issued the calm and unrest of beauty. In a sense other than that meant by our poet, Italy was gifted with that fatal dower of beauty, that inheritance in music to which here we wish specially to refer, which enabled those masters who came after Scarlatti to exalt their compositions as the models for European emulation. The aim of these Italian masters was frequently merely melodic, to the exclusion of that organic membering of parts without which music could not realize its power. The growth of the solo called into existence, as we have seen, the virtuosi, not seldom ungenerous, mean and intriguing, but wellnigh all-powerful to call down disastrous fate on any true musician who would not pander to their love of display and particular vanity. Overweening conceit induced many composers of ephemeral fame to look down upon those earnest spirits who turned from the prevailing methods to seek instruction and inspiration from those pure sources of art which the Netherlands and Italy had earlier afforded. Of these men, the modern ministers of consolation, Bach, Handel, Haydn, Gluck, Mozart, and Beethoven, who shall rightly speak? Truth herself shall testify of them, for, impelled by love, they sought and found her when her face was hidden through shame, and her eyes withholden from impurity.

But it has been rightly pointed out that even in this period of general deterioration there were numerous workers whose genius could not be vanquished by the false methods of their day. Many works have survived in which there are beautiful examples of melody and sentiment, and the skill of the virtuosi led doubtless to that desire for perfect rendering which now animates us, while the school for vocalization which the Italians established has trained the greatest of modern artists. Mozart, Handel, and Gluck availed themselves of Italian methods in song, whereas Bach was unacquainted with them. We see, then, in this eighteenth century a general decline in the lofty spirit of art, a general, but only general, decline in creative and inspiring thought. But if this is the general aspect, yet at this period there were in art, science, and literature the greatest prophets of the modern era. The eighteenth century was, in fact, a time of transition, of fructification and decay, as regards the methods which had advanced the human spirit onward to its goal of universal righteousness during the preceding centuries; but it was also the first century of the essentially modern spirit, the spirit of agonizing unrest striving to arrive at a knowledge of the truth. In fact, the thinkers of the eighteenth century kindled the fires of the social revolution which are burning more steadfastly, if less luridly, than ever to-day. The dream of liberty, fraternity, and equality is but the semblance of a more beautiful vision whose halo, cast around the tree at Calvary, has attracted, and will ever attract, the lofty spirits of the ages until the sacrifice of each for each shall indeed give us liberty, fraternity, and equality, though in a sense somewhat different to the

Precursors of the Great Tone Poets

appeal, ungoverned and misled, which rang in the ears of Europe at the time of the French Revolution.

This social revolution is, in fact, a fitting sequel to the awakening in art and literature to which we have alluded. Its moving spirit is the sanctity of humanity, the inherent rights of the individual, the case of the oppressed against the oppressor. The working out of such revolution must of necessity be attended with much ferment. Much that we have loved for the moment will be discarded, but it will be a loss in exchange for inestimable gain if the individual, when he has attained his status as such, shall desire righteousness, and not selfishness. But all great movements require expression in art. There must be some mediator who can articulate and present in noblest forms the aspirations and emotions of the unknown millions, so that they may recognise the ideal which is before, yet ever eludes, them.

The great artists and mediators of the present epoch have been and are musicians. Their brethren, the poets of a sister art, speak in their own particular tongue, but Music partakes of the nature of a universal language. If she lends her aid to words, they come home with accentuated force and an inner meaning which without her would have escaped us. If she speaks in her own accents we know and understand. But the great musicians have been and are most distinctly religious. From what source have the greatest tonal triumphs emanated? Whence have they derived their inspiration? Is it not from the Sacred Narrative and from revelation? This is a fact most important in an age such as this, when all men worthy of the name are in the death-throes with materialism. But the art is religious in a yet wider sense. She concerns herself with the whole range of life, all that has been, and she will enter with increasing sympathy into all that is to be. Can it be maintained that any other art thus illuminates and reconciles? Could any other art so illustrate, for instance, the creation of the world, the fall of man, his sorrow and despair, his ultimate victory in Christ? No! man is concerned to-day in a microscopic yet far-reaching investigation of all phenomena. The great philosophers have analyzed our emotions, as the great scientists have analyzed the material elements. Music can and does enter into every shade of subtle analysis, yet can combine her forces in a mighty tone torrent that is a reflection of almighty power. She has achieved through the burden of the ages, and having briefly mentioned the conditions surrounding those masters who raised her to such pre-eminence, let us see what manner of men they were, these mediators between the old and the new, these prophets and poets who, like the great Hebrews of old, seem ever to have stood in the presence of the Lord.

THE GREAT TONE POETS.

8—2

XXIII.

JOHANN SEBASTIAN BACH.

THE first tonal prophet and poet of the modern era, the era in which reason made tremendous protest against mere dogma, and the best religious instincts of human nature called imperatively for emancipation and for nearer individual contact with God, is Johann Sebastian Bach. We look dazzled at the brilliant victories of the Italian Renaissance, and amidst tumultuous beauty run riot with imagination we hear the voice of Savonarola at the close of the period uttering his lamentations.

The great Italian reformer saw and felt that in his own day and in his own country the glory and beauty of the movement had vanished in sensuality —that hardness of heart and indifference to primary human needs had diverted the waters of the Renaissance from their main fertilizing channel.

The deep need of the epoch was social, not mental, sociality in its widest sense: the right of the individual; his inherent majesty, which the accident of birth should not be able to impair—this and this only was the natural outcome of the new birth which came to humanity; this and this only was the sequel which German profundity and integrity, not Italian brilliancy and carelessness, placed before the mind of Europe.

The Reformation, then, this Protestantism, is distinctive of the new era. It was a protest, not only religious, as the word is usually applied, but scientific. It is the basis in the modern Western world of those laws of criticism which have submitted, or will submit, everything to searching analytical investigation, and as in the case of the natural world, so in the moral and ethical, men, by the light of revealed truth, or by those higher instincts of nobility which emanate from the Eternal Love, seek to apply to the reformation of society those principles of love, justice, and recompense which each would wish applied individually to self.

As an inspirer of thought and man of action the world has seen few such men as Luther. His genius, as it were, discovered and lay bare the inexhaustible treasures of the German language; his sympathy and genial humanity sent a thrill of song, poetical and tonal, throughout the Fatherland. He was the great awakener of German emotion. To Luther, a man who cared not for song was without the pale of humanity. But his enthusiasm was practical. In the Church, as we have seen, he gathered from all sources whatever was of the best and gave it to the people. In the schools he advocated the cause of song. In the streets the people needed not advocacy. Wherever two or three were gathered together, song was in the midst of them, and it is not too much to say that the Lutheran hymn was the saviour of German poetry, and a fount of German song. In the seventeenth century there was in Germany little poetry worthy of the name save that inspired by the devotional character of Luther's genius. His heir and successor in the realm of tone was Sebastian Bach.

True, two centuries had elapsed between the death of the great reformer in morals and the birth of the great reformer in tone; but the work of the latter could not have been without the former. The chorale was introduced by Luther; it was perfected by Bach. To what other influence than the Lutheran can we attribute the growth of Bach? Are there any other resources of German art and thought which can account for the advent of the great musician? In art Dürer stood by the side of Luther. In him again we find a man. Thought, thought ! help me to express my native thought. Teach me to express in my art the reality of Nature, its wonderful beauty, thrice beautiful to me an artist; the pathos of life, its realism, far apparently from the ideal, yet most precious to me as a man. This was the aim of Dürer, and he seems a man after Lutheran mould.

The aim of Dürer may be found in some respects in Bach's work, because both men were men of integrity, great and patient in soul. This, of course, is not to say that Bach was affected by Dürer, but is merely an endeavour to find what was noblest in Germany preceding Bach. One more allusion. In Bach's art we trace the mystic. Not shadowy outpourings of hysterical emotion, but beauties of eternal verities disclosed in vision —faint, it is true—to none save the noblest of mortals.

One such kindred spirit preceding Bach was Böhme, the father of German mysticism, the poor cobbler, whose soul lay far away in the regions of celestial love, and whose utterance is of the realities thereof. These three men, Luther, Dürer, Böhme, are those to whom the great musician Bach is akin, but he is truly the child of the former, and the father of the highest aspirations in instrumental music.

For confirmatory evidence we have only to trace the growth of the Bach family. The progenitor, Veit Bach, was born at Wechmar, near Gotha, in 1550, and, following his trade as a baker, settled, after considerable wanderings, near the Hungarian frontier. Veit Bach was a stanch Lutheran. Whether the Lutheran services had given him a love of music, or whether they had only quickened a constitutional sympathy, it is impossible to say. Certain it is that he was passionately fond of music, and, cast for a period among a population whose emotions found constant and ready utterance in tone, he brought back to Wechmar, whither he had returned on account of religious persecution, his beloved cythringa, and the art of playing it. There is evidence that this knowledge afforded him consolation and enjoyment in the quiet monotony of his life. While the mill was working, Veit Bach was often playing, and, doubtless, the peculiar charm and rhythm of old Hungarian melodies, songs of the people, which he had learned from the wandering gipsies, recurred to him, as well as those grand devotional hymns on which he had been nourished from childhood. We have said that Veit Bach was a stanch Lutheran. From father to son through generations the Lutheran doctrine, pure and undefiled, had been handed down, accompanied by the musical gift, until both uniting in Sebastian Bach, born at Eisenach in 1685, served to glorify the Lutheran chorale and the art which perfected it.

Again, the traditions of the great reformer must have been imbibed by Sebastian Bach from infancy. Surrounding his native town lay a circle of wooded heights, from one of which arose the Wartburg, that illustrious shrine of the German nation whither in mediæval and modern times her sons have repaired to exhibit and replenish their lamp of genius. There the minnesingers had gathered in contest of song; thither as a modern Elijah came the great monk, weary of soul, yet whose immortal genius unfolded the page of Sacred Writ; and down the wood-clad slope came issuing the melody of the Hebrew psalmist, translated into German speech, and entering into German hearts, mingled with the narrative of the Redeemer's passion lit by awful and solemn glory of Eternal Love. Who shall say that young Bach knew not of these things? Who will contend that, when his genius matured and ripened, the immortal tones in which the eternal passion was portrayed owed nothing to this sympathy of association, this spiritual life with the great reformer born two centuries before?

Yet once more. The Bach family was full of affection and sympathy one towards the other. Each year witnessed a reunion of the various members of the family scattered throughout Thuringia, and each came bearing the gift of music. As a child among the elders we can imagine how the young Sebastian revered his uncles, Johann Christopher and Michael Sebastian, in whom were conserved and developed the Lutheran tonal principles and traditions; how he somewhat feared the austere character of his elder brother, Johann Christopher, to whose charge he was entrusted upon the death of his father.

But we need not imagine how the soul of the young boy was filled with inexpressible yearning for the art of music. We know that it was so. His brother, who instructed him, gauged not the nature of the lad. Often and often did the boy's wistful eyes and loving heart covet the possession of a manuscript book kept by his brother in strict reserve, containing a priceless collection of compositions by the great German masters and mediators. The boy extracted them from their resting-place, and we see the young tone-prophet striving to master the art forms of Reinken, Buxtehude, Frescobaldi, Kerl, Froberger, and Pachelbel, endeavouring to wrest from them their style and inmost meaning by the light of the moon's pale rays, which led, alas! in after-years to blindness.

What revelations came to the soul of the young musician we know not. But his genius thus directed knew no pause until it had won for ever the freedom of the tonal art, until the last fetter of conventionality had been removed, until in all dignity and beauty music came forth, henceforth to comfort and solace the human heart. But of this anon. We trace the young boy to school; we see him a chorister in the choir of St. Michael's, Lüneberg. Here he entered the gymnasium, studying Greek and Latin, organ and violin playing. Here, too, he exhausted the treasures of the musical library. But at Hamburg the great Reinken was giving a series of organ recitals. Thither young Bach repaired. At Celle he became acquainted with several suites and other compositions of celebrated French masters. In 1703 he became violinist in the Saxe-Weimar orchestra, and in the same year, aged eighteen, he was appointed organist at the new church at Arnstadt, where other members of his family had held similar positions. Thus already we have ample evidence both of intense activity and catholicity of taste, and now, a mere youth, he enters upon his life-work, the perfecting of Church music, especially the chorale form, and the emancipation of the art from any influence whatsoever other than that it derives from contact with Nature and emotion. If we ask what equipment he had for this task, we answer enthusiasm, so deep, so tempered in all its qualities, that though in a few years he became the ablest performer of his time upon the harpsichord and organ, yet never once is the term virtuoso associated in our thought with the purity of aspiration which characterized him. His enthusiasm was religious, deep-seated, his vision far and wide, and no temporary triumph, no sunlit cloud of fame, could satisfy the imperative needs of his inmost nature. And this nature was calm with the calmness of strength, and with that tender purity and homely virtue which characterized the surroundings of his boyhood.

This enthusiasm, this religious instinct for what was noblest and best, led him early, as we have seen, to seek inspiration from the works of men who combined in their compositions all that the great previously existing schools had taught. Bach was never weary of learning, if perchance he could attain a more lucid or more beautiful expression of his thought. We have, then, this enthusiasm, this capacity for at once discerning what was best. Add to it one more quality, the religious, in its best sense, which young Bach possessed to the uttermost, the feeling that his art was but the medium of expression for the deep things of God, and we have the equipment with which the young musician started on his quest.

Young Bach had received no direct instruction in the schools of composition. That which he had he gathered with a catholicity of taste from all the renowned masters. Not one of his immediate ancestors had stirred beyond the confines of their simple home. Well for him was it so. No late meretricious Neapolitan tinsel could exist in the quiet calm beauty of his Thuringian dwelling-place. Nature lay before him. 'Come,' she said, 'seek to understand me. I have treasures that ye know not of, treasures that can only be gathered by the pure in heart and patient in spirit. Here around you, in your quiet German home, are the elements of all your strength. Here there is no distraction. Riches shall not allure you. Honourable poverty shall minister to your purity;' and young Bach knew that the voice was true, and, heeding it, there came to him likewise an inner voice, relating spiritual things, even as the voice of Nature related natural things.

Comprehending, then, his character, we pass on. His work at this period was formal. He felt, but could not express. But at Lübeck the noble-hearted Buxtehude was endeavouring to bring home to the hearts of the people the mission of music. Bach went thither. Fascinated by the grand organ-playing of the Lübeck master, and listening with heartfelt love to those memorable concerts of which we have previously spoken, Bach forgot both time and engagements.

Returning to Arnstadt, he was rebuked for his tardiness. But the spirit of Buxtehude was upon him. Henceforth the quiet people of Arnstadt knew no rest. Variations, subtle, beautiful, a refined and fuller contrapuntal treatment, mingled with the chorale. The conservatism of Arnstadt received a severe shock—a dreadful experience, doubtless, to the quiet German town. Such genius could come to no good end, and so the Consistory and Bach agreed to part.

We next find Bach at Mühlhausen, an old town not far from Eisenach. The choral singing of the church of St. Blasius, where Bach entered upon his duties as organist, had long been renowned, and Bach resolved to still further perfect the choral service. But his efforts met with no more encouragement than at Arnstadt, and the post of organist at Saxe-Weimar having been offered him, he accepted it.

Bach had married in October, 1707. In 1708, while at Mühlhausen, his first considerable work, composed for the Municipal Elector, appeared. His election at Saxe-Weimar was undoubtedly owing to his playing before the Duke Wilhelm

Ernst, and we can imagine with what pleasure the young musician, conscious of great power, looked forward to the intellectual and cultured life for which Weimar was renowned. In the course of a few years Bach was appointed orchestral and concert director to the Duke.

The liberal atmosphere of Weimar, the appreciation of men whose opinion was of worth, could but stimulate the mental faculties and widen the range of thought, and there is a breadth of conception and majesty in Bach at this period unknown before. With the assiduity of genius he laboured for the realization of his ideal. Palestrina, Lotti, and Caldara were laid under contribution. The master transcribed the works of these composers with his own hands, and arranged the violin concertos of Vivaldi for the harpsichord and organ. It is ever thus with the greatest artists. They assimilate all the forms of kindred art, yet never sacrifice their individuality. The means enabling them to express their inmost soul must be found, but their soul will alone dictate the form which its expression will assume. The chief compositions of Bach during his stay at Weimar were:

Three preludes in A minor, C, and G (4.13; 8.8, 11).

Three fugues in G minor, C, and G minor (4.7; 8.10, 12).

Fifteen preludes and fugues in A, F minor,

C minor, G minor, E minor, C, G, and D, besides a collection of eight shorter ones (2 3 5 6 ; 3 5 10 ; 4.2.3 ; 8.5.1—viii).

Three toccatas and fugues in F, C, and D minor (3.2, 8 ; 4.4).

Two fantasias and fugues both in C minor (3.6; 4.12); and three single works, namely, a fantasia in C (8.9); a pastorale in F (1.3); and the superb Passacaglio in C minor (1.2).*

The integrity of a great soul shines through all. But Bach is approaching the close of the first period of his career. An invitation has been given him—1717—to become conductor of the orchestra at the Court of Leopold of Anhalt Köthen, a prince remarkable for his benevolence and cultured attainments. Here his duties were comparatively slight, and his leisure abundant. Hitherto he had been engaged, as it were, in the Temple service. At Weimar he had developed into a great tone poet of sacred song. With refined strength and exquisite perception he had gathered up the related parts of song, weaving them into a unity of impassioned and majestic utterance.

But the great poet must have a wider experience. He must enter, as it were, into the great deeps of sacred emotion in things natural; he must perceive in the universe a deeper, a more majestic beauty even than in the Temple. Then

* See the 'Life of Sebastian Bach,' by Reginald Lane Poole, M.A., p. 40.

he will become a great prophet among his fellows, and illumine for all time the pathway of life, giving strength to the weak, consolation to the weary, and song to the blithe and pure of heart. This is what Bach became in tone. His attention at Köthen was directed mainly to instrumental music.

We have previously remarked upon the endeavours which certain German masters made to bring home to their countrymen an appreciation of instrumental music. How long the seed lay germinating in Bach's mind we know not. A new idea had taken possession of him, or, rather, he contemplated the application of the principle of his former labours in polyphony to instrumental music pure and simple.

At Köthen he supplemented his labours at Weimar. At Leipzig, whither we shall presently follow him, he brought them to completion.

But we are anticipating. We have traced for centuries the growth of polyphony in the various tone schools of Europe preceding and following the Renaissance. We have seen how patiently, how toilsomely, Music has broken one by one the fetters of conventionality—how she has grown in strength and beauty, anticipating the moment of her final deliverance. It has come at last. With the patience and impatience of genius Bach strikes in twain the last fetter of conventionality. He has realized his quest. The boy who, far away in future thought, studied the art forms of his great predecessors and contemporaries in the lowly chamber by the light of the silent moon has found his beloved, the Tonal Muse. She stands free before him to serve his will—his will purified by conception and incessant effort—and he will lead her in her new-found freedom and place her in the path of progress.

Bach's compositions at this time were:

A volume of six small easy preludes.
Fifteen inventions.
Fantasia and fugue in C minor, especially intended to exercise third and fourth fingers of both hands.
First part of 'Wohltemperirte Clavier.'
A book of instructions for beginners at the organ.
Six sonatas for violin and piano.
Nine trios for piano, flute and violin.
Four concertos for piano, with accompaniments for other instruments.
Six sonatas and trios for two pianos, with pedal obbligato.
Six concertos for different instruments, dedicated to the Markgraf of Brandenburg.*

The six small easy preludes and fifteen inventions he composed to serve as some slight introduction or preparation for one of the greatest of his works, the 'Wohltemperirte Clavier.' In this

* Extracted from Bitter's 'Life of Bach,' abridged translation by James E. Kay-Shuttleworth, pp. 35, 36.

latter work—the second part of which was composed at Leipzig—Bach attained the full mastery of form. The strivings and efforts of the great Netherland masters found completion in this work of Bach. In it is compressed the labours of centuries. The works of the masters Okeghem, Dufay, Josquin des Près, and others, are but prophecies in tone, announcing a realization of their ideal in the centuries yet to come, that ideal which they felt so particularly, yet could not express.

The evolution was certain, and it consummated in a kindred mind. The deepest expression of human feeling, the agony of the dire distress and conflict of life, the calm majesty of faith which enables the soul to overcome every obstacle, its pathetic appeal to God for rest and comfort, the strength of victory, are possible in music, are expressed in music as no other art can express them, because of Bach.

True to his trust, he extracted all that was best in the works of his predecessors and, vivifying it by his genius, created forms of expression which the greatest that have followed him have utilized and extolled.

But, as we have said, the great poet must perceive in things natural, in the beauty of the universe around him, in the sacred feelings of human emotion, a sacredness as worthy and as earnest, though less concentred in character, as that which exists in the more direct function of religious worship. To the great poet, however he works, all things are sacred. He it is who reveals the heaven that lies around us. He opens the portals of Nature, and we enter in to find strength and consolation.

Bach does all this in the masterly work we are considering. Not to the Italian, but to the German, did Nature at length disclose her choicest method of expression, and this because the German had ever lived in close contact with her. In all Bach's works at this period the work of emancipation goes forward. Take, for instance, the Brandenburg concertos leading to the combination of the present orchestra.

But a new sphere of action here again opens to Bach. His master and friend, the Prince of Köthen, was distracted from the pursuit of music by his wife's want of interest therein, and so Bach sorrowfully looks around him for a more congenial appointment. This he found at Leipzig as Cantor to the school of St. Thomas. Leipzig, like Weimar, was celebrated for its intellectual life; but the various vexations which the great musician encountered from the action of the authorities reflects but little credit upon them. Bach's labours here were simply titanic. There were four churches at Leipzig, the principal being St. Nicholas and St. Thomas. Bach seems to have been responsible for the musical service at each. How innate and healthy was his genius may be inferred from the fact that for these musical services alone 380 cantatas seem to have been composed. Bach entered upon his labours at Leipzig at the age of thirty-eight, and continued therein until his death in 1750. Let us examine briefly the nature of these labours, and endeavour to glean from them their characteristic principles.

When Bach came to Leipzig, he came full of experience and power. As a youth he had devoted himself to the perfecting of Church music. Untiringly, unceasingly, with steadfast love, he had brought the laws of counterpoint and fugue to mingle with the grace of melody and the genius of a noble imagination. At Köthen his poetic and artistic temperament roamed through the realms of Nature, and brought us near to the understanding of their varied utterance. At Leipzig he finished the education of his life and his career as a tone poet. He seeks again the shelter of the Temple, but his genius has matured and ripened. He has examined the mysteries of life. His enthusiasm for the pure and good is stronger than ever, but life is still a mystery. Evil, pain, love deep as hell and high as heaven, the titanic conflict of opposing principles, Nature and her decrees, sorrow, remorse, sweet unaffected joy, and tranquil resignation—what mean they all? The answer, the solution, is on Calvary. There is no other solution. Intellect, deny it how it will, is baffled by the complex problem. The solution is of love through trouble and anguish. The Passion music of Bach rises to the sublime understanding of this grand mystery, and again the evolution of the old mystery and passion play consummates in a kindred mind. Again the triumph of faith is with the German. Luther frees the understanding from tyranny. Bach raises it to the region of genius and sympathy, and closes the labours of a thousand years of Christian tonal effort by this Passion music of the Redeemer. But while this is so, he initiated the modern period of tonal art, leaving, however, this Passion music as his noblest legacy, as if to warn men that no other solution of life exists.

But, though Bach's genius was thus supreme, it was not because he was undisturbed by the vexations of daily life. Rarely, if ever, has an artist equally great produced in such boundless profusion the highest works of genius, when engaged with men most frequently unable to understand his thought, and immersed in the arduous duties of teacher in an art noteworthy for producing fatigue and exhaustion of spirit. But his enthusiasm and strength were equal to the task. With grand integrity, and desire for the welfare of the congregations of the churches alluded to, he obtained from their respective ministers the texts of their discourses for the ensuing Sundays, and produced, apparently without effort, hundreds of cantatas, to convey to the hearers the inner meaning of the words which fell from the preachers' lips. These cantatas frequently opened with orchestral introduction followed by a chorus, usually very impressive, and imbued with the meaning of the text. The recitatives and solo airs would still further convey this meaning, while a chorale or hymn in four parts, with elaborate instrumental accompaniment, served to express the feelings of the whole congregation. To each instrument was assigned a separate part, and the whole accompaniment was separate from the singing.

But if Bach in the consummation of the chorale perfected Luther's work in the realm of music, he in his Passion music finds worthy expression of a nation's devotion. His genius, as it were, felt the spirit-life of the past. His soul vibrated to the yearnings of the unknown millions of his race who had passed away in the centuries preceding him, and whose consolation in their humble toil, in the various hardships of their lives, was the narrative of this Passion music of the Saviour Christ. The rough, dramatic presentation accorded to this narrative gathered as time went on elements of beauty and traditional treatment around it. It was powerfully to affect the drama proper and oratorio, but in its direct and proper functions it was to inspire the first, and in some respects the greatest, of the great musicians of Germany to his utmost effort, to his most lofty flight of genius, as his winged spirit soared through the ages of the past toward the future of ages yet to come.

This Passion music of St. Matthew is the noblest presentment of the characteristics of the German mind, and is unsurpassed in the realm of religious art. It is an unfolding of the German spirit, and evidences qualities the possession of which make for national greatness.

As we have said, Bach is the great lyric poet of his nation, the first great German genius after the devastating horrors of war. Looming on the sight, or as contemporaries, are Handel, Leibnitz, Wolf, Klopstock, Lessing, and Winckelmann. The modern era, with its philosophy and revolution, has arrived. The domain of thought is enwidened, and the Middle Ages blend and fade in the historic vista of the past. But the modern era commences with these great affirmations in art and poetry. Bach takes the narrative of the Passion, and erects the Cross anew with sympathetic genius of art and love. Handel, as if he had caught Isaiah's prophetic fire, gave to Europe its most beautiful and noble epic, the 'Messiah,' and Klopstock, the first of the great line of Germany's modern poets, devoted his genius and labour to the same subject. But with Bach and Handel no miserable conflicting elements of theology sully the conception of the Saviour Christ. Though Protestant, these great artists rise to the universal and the true. The highest art is absolute and knows no appeal. It is in harmony with universal law, both spiritual and physical. With these remarks we pass to consider the genius of Handel.

XXIV.

HANDEL.

IN studying the life and works of Johann Sebastian Bach, we have traced, as it were, the evolution of a supreme artist. The various influences which united in his art unfold themselves with a regular and beautiful sequence, and present one of the most fascinating examples of the growth of an artistic spirit. He was born to a rich inheritance in art, the pride and glory of a noble and virtuous ancestry, and he was at once the tonal poet of the past and the prophet of a far-reaching future. He succeeded to his kingdom by birthright, but Handel, his great contemporary, took his by storm.

Such are the manifestations of genius. If in one instance we can trace the mental and spiritual influences which result in highest excellence, in another analysis avails us nothing. The artist who may be the subject of contemplation is simply born with predetermined faculties, and becomes in his peculiar method supreme. We rightly say of such an one that his genius is heaven-born. Thus it was with Handel. But though science may not in all cases enable us to connect cause and result, yet, with regard to genius, we feel that such manifestation is not the result of chance—that qualities so allied to the Divine do not appear haphazard, but are necessary factors at their actual time of appearing to inspire humanity with a nobler mission, to interpret to it its past thought, or to clothe in some new form the eternal and cardinal principles of beauty, both concrete and abstract.

Thus with Bach and Handel, the one the great lyric, the other the great epic, master of his epoch. Think, was it merely chance that these men were born where they were, when they were, and for the purpose which each was to fulfil? Surely not, if we study the progress of humanity. They were necessary to stimulate the artistic faculties of Europe in a new direction, they were necessary for the interpretation of its past thought, they were necessary for the affirmation of great religious truths when the revelation of the material world was about to fill the mind of Europe, and to enter apparently, but not in reality, into conflict with the spiritual.

The age of the great scientists in morals and physics was approaching, both necessary and excellent in the realm of universal thought. There were to be dreamers also who were to dream dreams, containing, as some dreams do, such elements of beauty and truth as, issuing upon the awakening sense, should cause transformation in modern life. This intellectual commotion demanded a spiritual equilibrium, while, by contrast, certain phases of thought of the eighteenth century, inert and paralyzed, required momentum, and of the great artists and thinkers who were to arise in Europe to control the destinies of its future thought, Bach and Handel take place amongst the glorious forerunners. Their leaven of beauty has leavened the whole lump.

Both were born in the province of Thuringia, Bach, as we have seen, at Eisenach, Handel at Halle, February 23, 1685, twenty-seven days previously to his great contemporary. But though Handel is the elder of the two, yet he seems nearer to us than Bach. This is because he is endowed more distinctly with the modern spirit. His works, too, found a readier and wider acceptation than those of his gifted fellow-countryman. It has only been recently that the beauty, depth, and breadth of the Leipzig master have become known, but to know is to love and reverence. In his works are no fugitive elements. They represent a beautiful unity, and are in music what the great Gothic cathedrals are in architecture—an expression of the yearnings of men's hearts for the completion of their nature in spiritual love.

No purer artist ever lived than Bach. Content and calm, he wrought for his God and for his art. In him we see the full effects of inherited capacity and genius. The great mediator between the old and modern schools, he consummated in himself the requirements of ages, and gave powerful stimulus to those which were to follow. Subjective, rising from the individual to the universal, deeply analytical, yet, when occasion demanded, unsurpassed in intensity of dramatic conception and winged might, he presents the most striking contrast, both in his character and in his art, with the musician whose works we are about to consider.

Like Bach, Handel was nurtured in a robust Lutheranism. We have seen how subtle were the influences which streamed into Bach's soul from this source, but Handel represents its different qualities. His conception and his sympathy dwelt on those episodes in human history distinguished by their pathetic nature and development, which resulted in the grand spectacle of national or individual heroism. In the delineation of such incidents he is unequalled, and this is so because no artist has been possessed, if the term be admissible, of so grand and historic an objective sense. If we wish to realize the majesty of his nature, we must do so in the marvellous breadth and power of his choruses. If we wish to understand how simple and full of love, we must listen to those exquisite melodies, so freely interspersed throughout his works, which are either the simplest expression of a winged brightness, so radiant, so full of unlimited prophecy and hope, or else the sighing forth of the deeps of the human heart when even suffering has ceased to pain, when the bruised spirit is only able to believe, and resignation but remains, holy and calm in its desolation.

But whatever the incident, Handel feels, thinks, and suffers as a hero. We shall see how wonderful is the influence of one inspired genius upon another as we follow the details of Handel's life; how time and distance fade and kindred souls embrace, and find completion in each other across the lapse of ages, though century after century intervene, though race and climate differ, though the civilization peculiar to the one has passed away, and that which nurtureth the other has but dawned. In the realm of genius these things are as though they were not. Handel's great epic, the 'Messiah,' is but the completion of Isaiah's prophetic utterance. German and English life has been cradled in the genius of Israel, and the prophet and the poet have brought home the message of consolation to many a weary soul among the sons of men.

It is not necessary to trace with much detail the events of Handel's life previous to his arrival in this country. Born of parents who were possessed with the qualities of vigour and common-sense, though, so far as is ascertained, without any musical capacities, Handel, from the dawn of consciousness, lived in and for music. The passion growing with his childish years, the father, who had other designs for his son, placed in his way every obstacle. In vain, the child's will was the stronger, and the incident which led to the intervention of the Duke of Weissenfels virtually decided little Handel's career. Placed under Zachau of Halle, he soon outstripped his master, and later took prominent position in the musical life of his native city. But his enterprising spirit yearned for a wider arena, and, a mere youth, he started for Hamburg, attracted thither by the fame of German opera. Engaged in the orchestra as second violin, his talents were quickly discerned by one Matheson, a young man of somewhat brilliant though superficial parts. Their friendship conferred mutual artistic benefits. Here Handel learned the elements of his art, and produced several operas in the prevailing method —a hybrid combination of German and Italian— with success. These operas contain indications of that gift for melodic writing for which, subsequently, he became so distinguished, but otherwise call for no remark. It was here, likewise, he composed the Passion music of St. John, which, with Keiser's ' Blütige und sterbende Jesus,' marked a new departure from traditional methods.

The opera at Hamburg soon declined, under the erratic guidance of Keiser, and we can well imagine that the idea proffered to Handel by Prince Gaston de Medici, brother of the Grand-Duke of Tuscany, needed but suggestion for adoption. Accordingly, having paid a farewell visit to his mother, it is probable that Handel arrived at Florence very early in the year 1707. If Florence was really the first city he visited, it was indeed an appropriate circumstance, for was it not here that the gifted circle of dilettanti, in their endeavour to supply suitable music for the Greek drama, evolved the dramatic recitative from which sprang opera seria and the oratorio, both of which forms Handel essayed, and in one of which he will ever remain unapproached.

How delightful and congenial his visit we can well imagine. Endowed with great mental gifts, and possessed of a handsome person, he united in himself both dignity and independence. No untoward incident marred the brilliancy of his reception, no alien element obtruded into those conceptions of beauty and genius which must have crowded thick and fast upon a mind so capable of bringing them to good effect. At short intervals Handel visited the centres of intellectual life and genius of Italy—Florence, Rome, Naples, Venice. What names are these! and each must have bestowed upon the artist its peculiar mental and characteristic charms. At Rome the Scarlattis, Alessandro and Domenico, received him with brotherly affection. The amiable and gifted Corelli sought to enter into the spirit of his compositions. That aristocracy of intellect and birth, the Arcadia, welcomed with hearty welcome the musician and the man. Surely it is to the credit of Italy that she gave such generous reception to German genius.

Handel's compositions whilst in Italy may be thus enumerated :

In 1707, at Rome, a 'Laudate,' and a 'Dixit Dominus' in Latin, taken from Psalm cx.

In 1708 'La Resurrezione' in Italian.

In the same year ' Il Trionfo del Tempo e del Disinganno.'

At Florence, in 1707, he produced ' Rodrigo.'

In Venice, in 1708, ' Agrippina.'

At Naples he produced the pastoral play ' Aci, Galatea e Polifemo,' written in the form of a cantata, which, however, must not be confounded with the later work on the same subject.

His stay extended to about three years ; and the question now arises, what were the precise artistic benefits which Handel derived from such a truly liberal education?

If we study his method at Hamburg, then his opera ' Rodrigo,' then the later opera ' Agrippina,' and the ' La Resurrezione,' we shall find a continuous development in orchestral resources. His work at Hamburg was naturally conventional, though containing here and there numbers of remarkable melodic beauty, but the orchestration was very scant. In 'Rodrigo' much of his Hamburg work was embodied ; but more important than all else, Handel was learning the secret of writing for the voice.

In 'Agrippina' and 'La Resurrezione' there is

a greater advance in orchestration, especially in the latter; but, as we have stated, more important than the science of orchestral effect was the experience that Handel gained by writing effectively for the voice. He ever possessed a natural melodic gift, but he needed the knowledge of Italian methods, and the stimulus of writing for renowned artists, to exalt this gift into the most conspicuous characteristic of his genius.

Leaving Italy in the autumn of 1709, Handel visited his family, and then proceeded to Hanover. Here, after much hesitation, he consented to succeed Steffani, capellmeister to the Elector, afterwards George I. of England, and, having been granted a year's leave of absence, we find him in London in the autumn of 1710.

Probably in the whole history of English art no parallel could be found where the influence arising from the visit of a foreigner was so memorable or so lasting. It would seem, looking not merely to the effects which Handel's genius was to exert upon the future of his art, as such, but regarding the influence which he has exerted upon the national life through the medium of families innumerable, who for a century have lovingly performed his works, that his residence was ordained in a country where, it will be my endeavour subsequently to show, the elements only existed for the development and manifestation of his power to aid and encourage, with many other similar influences coming to the birth, that glorious moral life which dawned again for England in the eighteenth century, and whose sequel is the grand social deliverance of our own day.

But before we study the peculiar thought and characteristics of the eighteenth century we will first briefly speak of Handel's efforts and triumphs in opera, for it was through this medium and his art education therein that he became the great master of oratorio.

At Handel's advent dramatic music in England was a mixture of feebleness and incoherence. Less than two decades previously death had claimed the one musician, Henry Purcell, whose genius could alone have created a national school, and between this sad event and Handel's arrival in this country there occurred a dreary interregnum, in which the efforts made to introduce operatic music were quite unworthy, and whose absurdities called forth the sarcastic indignation of Addison. However, there was a passionate desire for opera of some description, fostered doubtless by wealthy and learned travellers who had returned from Italy, and in 1709, on the occasion of the production of Scarlatti's 'Pyrrhus and Demetrius,' the English public had the pleasure of listening to the renowned Nicolini, the first Italian singer of real genius who had appeared before it. Even Addison bore testimony to the merits of this artist. It is easily imaginable, then, with what impatience the first opera from Handel was awaited. He was equally impatient, and with a wonderful rapidity he produced 'Rinaldo,' which, it is true, contained some of his previous compositions, notably the ever beautiful air 'Lascia ch' io pianga,' which had already appeared in the 'Trionfo del Tempo,' and was originally an instrumental sarabande in 'Almira.'

The success of this opera was great and deserved. With one supreme, brilliant, and rapid effort Handel's genius attained its fulness in this class of composition; for, as a whole, 'Rinaldo' was never surpassed by his later operas. True, experience came with the many years of passionate striving and effort which yet lay before the maestro; gem after gem of beauteous song was to be set in emotional splendour throughout the many operas which Handel produced for thirty years; but no real advance was made in the form of the art, only a fuller employment of orchestral and vocal resources which the artist had at his command.

The reform of opera, and the breaking of the tyranny of Italian methods—its growth into an artistic unity excluding the vanity of singers, and the irrelevancy in the unfolding of its various incidents—were to be entrusted to the peculiar genius of Gluck. But looking to Italian opera, as such, no master, either before or after Handel, can be said to excel him.

Shortly after the production of 'Rinaldo,'

Handel

Handel returned to Hanover; but after a stay of sixteen months we again find him in London at the end of 1712. His permanent residence in this country now commenced, notwithstanding the capellmeistership at Hanover, and his reappearance was signalized by the production of 'Pastor Fido' (November 26).

And now for a number of years this great man poured forth opera after opera. Now idolized by the public, now left in neglect, the subject of well-nigh unlimited admiration and abuse, engaged in factions with his singers and with rivals of unquestioned talent, the giant spirit never falters. Health may fail, and reason herself be imperilled by the herculean nature of his struggles, the tumults of his victories and defeats, but the will is absolute, undaunted. The heroic spirit of the man must find the measure of its utterance; and when all seems lost, and Italian opera lies bankrupt and beggared, the master with supreme genius creates and extols to highest place amongst sacred art the noble and majestic form of oratorio.

Thus, while engaged in composing his numerous operas, of which the chief are:

'Rinaldo,'
'Radamisto,'
'Ottone,'
'Giulio Cesare,'

he was producing, collaterally, and at different intervals, a series of works which indicated the true nature of his genius, and whose sequel was the long roll of imperishable oratorios.

The works thus indicated are the Utrecht 'Te Deum' and 'Jubilate,' the 'Chandos Anthems,' the beautiful pastoral of 'Acis and Galatea,' and the first of the oratorios called 'Esther.' In these the Handel known to the majority of Englishmen discloses himself.

His residence at Cannons, the seat of James, Duke of Chandos, afforded him repose from the worries of an assertive artistic career, and in this atmosphere of calm and culture were fostered those art germs which, fructified by experience in opera, expanded into the beauty of the 'Messiah' and the majesty of 'Israel in Egypt.'

It was, however, many years before Handel would yield obedience to those reserve faculties which were to create the epic in musical art. Had fortune uniformly smiled upon the master, and the English public appreciated his predilection for opera, the result would have been lamentable. But faction and ennui wrought disaster. After years of striving Handel had the mortification to find himself deserted and bankrupt. The 'Beggar's Opera' proved the *coup de grace*, and demonstrated the desire of the English public for an art form either of native growth or sympathetic to the national taste.

From a cursory glance at English society at this period, one might be tempted to ask where existed the sustaining power which made oratorio the most characteristic expression of our emotion, and which, though finding utterance through a foreign artist, was so great, so powerful, that Handel in the realm of art occupies the most prominent position amongst us, is most closely allied to us in spirit.

Handel is to us in Music what Milton is in Poetry. Both worked on the moral impulses of the nation. Both were noble in manhood and majestic in conception. Both possessed unbounded faith in the scheme of man's redemption. Art was to Handel, in the religious sphere, an expression of innermost conviction, not merely a great intellectual capacity to receive and reissue emotion. It was the soul of the man paying noblest homage to its Maker; and it was a similar religious feeling, mingling with that moral earnestness and emotion springing up from several sources at this period, which was to transform the life of England internally and enlarge her boundaries well-nigh indefinitely externally.

Beneath the cynicism of politics personified by Walpole; beneath those interminable wrangles of eminent divines who illustrated their mission, not infrequently, by a general brutality of expression towards their opponents, and their fervid faith by banishing God into a cloudland of metaphysics; beneath the scepticism of the age which culminated in Hume's philosophy of negation and Swift's savage misanthropy; when religion, in fact, was made the occasion of intellectual gladiatorial display, there were coming to the birth the most beautiful and salutary influences in English life.

The brothers Wesley were the great awakeners of this moral conviction which has made England mainly Liberal in politics, which transformed the national poetry from a frigid classicism represented by Dryden and Pope into the spontaneous utterance of the more genial impulse of humanity, whose first exponent was Cowper and whose greatest is Wordsworth. The religion by which these two modern apostles reanimated the English race gained, through Burke and Wilberforce, its greatest triumph in the emancipation of the negro. 'Faith, faith; give us a living faith!' was the groan throughout the length and breadth of England in Handel's day, and to it art responded, ' I know that my Redeemer liveth.'

The 'Messiah' was brought home to the hearts of England as Isaiah had implanted its desire in the hearts of Israel. The prophet and the artist-poet mingled in spirit, and never has prophecy found a more ample or more beautiful expression. But how, according to the canons of art, was this expression possible? We have seen that it came to be triumphant because the religious sense of England demanded it. Let us study the manner of its evolution, and note how Handel's exertions in opera were wrought into the result.

We have already, when speaking of the Monodic School, which had its origin in the intellectual and artistic yearnings of the Florentine dilettanti, described how opera and oratorio were the mental children of such intellectual and artistic commingling. We have also seen how Carissimi was the first to unite a beautiful and appropriate music to the verbal narrative, and atone in some measure for the loss which befell in the art of polyphonic writing.

Until the time of Carissimi, oratorio as well as opera was spectacular; but gradually the divergence in their emotional capacity and character manifested itself, and spectacular presentation in oratorio began to decline. Alessandro Scarlatti, Caldara, Colonna, Leo, and Stradella, were the successors of Carissimi, and each, according to his special gift, modified, ennobled, and established certain characteristics of the art form we are considering. Handel's Italian oratorio, ' La Resurrezione,' belongs to the same period as Stradella's singular and beautiful masterpiece, ' San Giovanni Battista,' which was performed at the church of St. John Lateran about 1676.

This work may be considered as the finest example of oratorio produced previous to Handel's great conceptions.; but in these conceptions mingled elements from which the Italian nation was excluded. These elements were no less than that wonderful religious feeling which Germany alone could supply—which only those who had been fed upon the milk and honey of the Reformation could possess, and that direct utterance, that breadth, power, and simple majesty which was the characteristic of English sacred music.

Handel was indebted to Purcell's mode of expression in the Utrecht 'Te Deum' and 'Jubilate.' His genius was his own, and how nobly that genius developed is shown in the 'Chandos Anthems,' which, as we have already said, were the precursors of the oratorios. But in these latter was yet another element, and that Italian. It was no less than the total experience of Handel's exertions in opera; it was no less than that mastery of expression of every human emotion so freely manifested in such creations as 'Rinaldo' and 'Radamisto.' And thus Handel's pre-eminence in oratorio was no spasm of genius, but an organic growth, most marvellous, it is true, because of the wonderful soil in which it developed.

In the Italian opera certain forms of composition had of necessity to be observed. Such forms were

> The Aria Cantabile,
> Aria di Portamento,
> The Aria di mezzo Carattere,
> Aria Parlante,
> Aria di Bravura,

and these were boldly transferred by Handel into the structure of oratorio. His genius sublimated these forms, and gave them an expression according to their individual character, unsurpassed and unsurpassable.

Consider, for instance, the examples, 'Angels ever bright and fair,' 'I know that my Redeemer liveth,' 'Waft her, angels, through the skies,' 'He was despised and rejected,' and 'Rejoice greatly,' each of which may be referred to one or other of the forms mentioned, and the dullest can understand how great was the debt Handel owed to his training in opera. But there was one species of composition in which he was not bound by any method of traditional treatment, in which, too, he greatly delighted, and in which all the resources of his marvellous contrapuntal skill in writing in facile progression for the voice were displayed. No master has ever wielded such power in choruses as Handel. He gathers up all his resources, and utilizes them to enforce some peculiar lesson, to moralize upon consequences, to depict with the full force of dramatic passion certain episodes, or to illustrate by analogy certain events. Such choruses are:

'Envy, eldest born of hell,'
'Is there a man,' } in 'Saul.'
'O fatal consequence of rage '
'Help, help the king ' (' Belshazzar '),
'We come in bright array ' ('Judas Maccabæus').
'He gave them hailstones,'

and others.*

The years between the performance of 'The Beggar's Opera,' 1728 and 1740, when Handel finally quitted the field of operatic writing, were the most strenuous in his career. Fashion, envy,

* See article 'Oratorio' in Grove's 'Dictionary of Music.'

disease and financial disaster seemed, as it were, to combine to crush the energies and spirit of the man who had laboured so faithfully to educate English taste in music. But, however embittered were these years, they were full of incessant effort, and witnessed the production of some of the most beautiful of Handel's operatic writing, the noble music set to Dryden's ode in celebration of St. Cecilia's Day, entitled 'Alexander's Feast,' and a variety of instrumental compositions.

Equally important and of great influence over Handel's future was the performance, not at first by himself, of 'Acis and Galatea,' and the oratorio 'Esther,' both composed years previously at Cannons. The appreciation manifested at the simple beauty and majesty of these works showed clearly the current of English taste, and, though Handel clung with desperate tenacity to opera, he yielded at last to the force of circumstances and the latent power of his genius. With sublime grandeur he burst into the realm of oratorio by the production of 'Saul' and 'Israel in Egypt.' Both these masterpieces were composed between July 23 and October 11, 1738. The first was produced on January 16, 1739, and the last on April 4 of the same year.

And now we have merely to stand by and relate the triumphs of a unique genius; to feel, to follow its sympathy with all that was noble and beautiful in human history; to stand wondering at the majestic flight of its conception, to marvel at its consummate ease and mastery of expression.

My task in this essay has been merely to show the evolution of Handel's art life, to trace, if it might be, the manifold causes which made Handel the greatest master of oratorio. But one feels that the oratorio the 'Messiah' is not merely an art work, but a summing up in art, a new cry unto heaven and a rejoicing before it, of the ancient and modern spirit—a mingling of the inspiration of the East and the genius of the West. It is the song of prophecy and a praise pæan in its accomplishment. In no other work of genius is the beauty of Israel and its influence over the West so clearly, so grandly shown.

The noble heart of Isaiah is full of agonizing grief for the sin of Israel. His prophetic vision sees the decay of empires that border and depress his beloved land. His nation has forsaken the way of the Lord, and what comfort is there remaining? Yea, to the beautiful and pure there is comfort, and it is in the revelation of righteousness. With what exquisite pathos Handel interprets this message of comfort! 'Comfort ye, comfort ye My people, saith your God. Speak ye comfortably to Jerusalem, that her warfare is accomplished, that her iniquity is pardoned.' And then follows the joy and glory of the whole earth attendant upon this revelation. Not only Isaiah, but Malachi, and Zechariah take up the parable of the Lord's appearing, and before these the great singer of Israel and its musician-king had also felt the certainty of glory that was to issue from his native Bethlehem; and centuries before him, in the dim distance of Eastern thought, but in imperishable conviction of imperishable life, the patriarch Job affirmed that the Redeemer liveth. But if this seer of the East and Israel's prophets proclaim the revelation of the Divine Love, to the Evangelists and Apostles is left the imperative and glorious duty of spreading the realization of fulfilment. St. Luke bears witness to it, the noble-hearted Paul preaches it at Corinth and at Rome, while from the Isle of Patmos there arises from the beloved Apostle and seer a transcendent glory of speech and utterance, and hallelujahs resound throughout earth and heaven, and before the throne of the King of kings for ever and ever.

All this has Handel translated into tone as he alone could translate it. Say not that genius is circumscribed, that the soul of man of necessity has not fellowship with the noblest of the past; say not, too, that this man was not beloved of the Lord, for he likewise was a prophet, though in tone—a seer of visions, and one filled with the melody of life. He had a great message to deliver, and was found equal to it—the same message which, wafted from Israel's shores, has filled the West with glory and the energy of love. Was it not, and is, that the Redeemer liveth, and that He shall reign for ever and ever? Hallelujah and amen.

Handel lies buried at Westminster, but his genius is an increasingly living force amongst us.

XXV.

GLUCK.

IN our slight contemplation of the works of Bach and Handel we have been conscious of contact with two of the noblest spirits of their time. Theirs was the supreme happiness of expressing in their art the deep-felt yearning of the soul for communion with God; of bequeathing to humanity a medium of expression for deepest religious feeling. They dwelt in that serener air which encircles the throne of everlasting truth; their song is the song of the soul assured. But if they represent, and worthily fulfilled, the pure and vigorous faith of the era in which they lived, yet there were other elements, other emotions, surging with hot passion in the minds of men.

The awakening of Europe in the Renaissance had not been an awakening to beauty of form alone. There had also been a revelation of social rights, the kindling of the intellect to examine with the ray of reason the conditions and aim of existence. It was a moment of supreme import to modern Europe—the first moment, as it were, of conscious outlook upon the deep mysteries of the universal life. The heavens and the earth were indeed declaring the glory of God. The revelation of the laws of the universe flashed upon the mind of man. He found himself in a new inheritance, but he found also the cares incident thereupon.

Acute minds scanned with closest scrutiny the origin of all things. No institution was sacred; no creed of necessity inviolate. Where was the fundamental condition of things, what the elemental passions, where could be discerned the law of unity connecting the human with the Divine? Historians, philosophers, poets, in turn essayed the answer, and from their labours has resulted that nobler comprehension of the universe which is our inheritance to-day.

The great discovery was, so to speak, the unity of life. The voice of a narrow theology grew feeble beside the utterance of the new word of God—that word which came not only from nature, but from remote nations, who, as men began to discern, were nobler in their majestic expression of primal affection and passion, in the glory of their manhood in fact, than the examples of that stultified life of affectation and asceticism, not seldom of hypocrisy and vice, which a dogmatic theology, temporizing between earth and heaven, held up as highest ideal. Men were growing weary of affectation, whether in Church,

State, or social life. Art also was growing weary, and music, the most subtle in her interpretation of life, found her utterance stifled, her powers denied, in the prevalent method of Italian opera.

On July 2, 1714, at Weidenwang, near Neumarkt, was born the musician Christopher Willibald Gluck, whose glory it was that he overthrew the existing methods of the Italian school, and with pure æsthetic sense, educated by the masterpieces of Greek tragedy, swept away all puerile affectation, and elevated dramatic music to be the faithful interpreter of the various passions of man's soul and heart. Although of humble origin, he had the advantage of an excellent training under the care of the Jesuits, and received instruction in singing, also lessons on the organ and harpsichord. From the Jesuit seminary he went to Prague, and from thence to Vienna. At the latter city he became acquainted with Prince Melzi of Lombardy, and returned with him to Italy, 1737-1738. At this period he placed himself under the care of the celebrated teacher of counterpoint, Giovanni Battista Sammartini of Milan, and having studied the principles of his art under this master for four years, produced his first opera, 'Artaserse,' at Milan, 1741.

Then followed a number of operas, which were neither better nor worse than the usual *opera seria* of the period. But of whatever merit, they served, by establishing his fame, to gain an invitation to visit the Haymarket Opera House in

London, 1745. This was the critical moment of Gluck's career. His receptive nature lay open to receive impressions, his genius to be guided by principles which circumstances would in part determine. These circumstances were fortunate, for Gluck had the opportunity of hearing in Handel's oratorios with what exquisite fidelity and majesty the deepest emotions of the heart could be portrayed. A new light as to the nature and mission of dramatic music dawned upon the young master. There was wrought within him a fuller consciousness of the ideal to be attained. He discerned that there must be no incongruity in presentment of opera. Unity of time, place and action were of vital consequence, and this unity could not be broken, as had been hitherto the case, to exhibit the peculiar vanity of singers. At Paris also, whither he proceeded from London, he gained a new insight into the principles of his art. He came under the influence of Rameau, and the concise character of his recitative, and his principles of musical declamation, were not lost upon him. Time and contemplation, however, were necessary for the growth of his artistic spirit, for his mental conceptions to receive adequate fulfilment through the medium and mastery of the forms of art. With a mind thus enriched by experience, and a genius enkindled by contact with other spirits, Gluck returned to Vienna, 1746. For many years the growth and assimilation of ideas went silently onward — ideas of the majesty and humanity of the classic spirit, which were likewise awakening in the minds of great art students and critics such as Winckelmann and Lessing. Occasionally this æsthetic quiet was broken by visits to Naples, Rome, and Bologna, to conduct one or other of the operas he had written; yet, although in these may be found indications of his future art methods, there was no decided breaking with the traditions of the past, no sustained effort to develop and continue the great dramatic principles first outlined by Jacopo Peri in his 'Eurydice,' produced at Florence a century and a half before. In the fervent pursuit of the classic ideal the keen intellectual Florentines had divined the true art principles of dramatic music, and now, when the methods of exposition were so much better known, when the capabilities of expression according to the technique of art had been so much increased, there flowed from the mind of Gluck his immortal 'Orfeo,' which, like all great works of genius, was well-nigh unconscious in its outflowing, but which most consciously portrayed the deep imbibing of the grandeur and beauty of Attic tragedy.

Often and often had despairing musicians, captivated by the lofty passion, the deep love, the human tenderness, which thrills through every line of this masterpiece of Euripides, sought to enhance its wondrous beauty by appropriate musical setting. But the time was not yet. The modern spirit had to feel its kinship with that long-lost heroic beauty, with that single imperative utterance from the heart's deeps of passionate emotion. And now the time had come. The apostles of the natural in Western Europe had sent an electric thrill of primal sympathy through the formal atmosphere of etiquette and conventionality, and Gluck, whether he knew it or not, in accord therewith, took Vienna by storm with the production of his 'Orfeo,' October 5, 1762. At last in musical art was consummated the union of the classic with the modern spirit. At last, with adequate and simple majesty, the musician could unfold the burden of the poet. A wise restraint is one of the chief characteristics of this great work. Preceded by an overture intended as a characteristic epitome, the opera, in number after number, displays the earnest desire of the musician to support the text. The music is a loving ally, not a competitor, enhancing by qualities peculiarly its own the sublimity of the poem. An orchestral background supports with vivid tone-colour the effects of scenic presentation, while the appropriate introduction of choruses and concerted pieces welds into compact and organic art-unity the entire production. It is easy to understand the profound impression which this departure in operatic writing must have produced. Melody, for its merely sensuous effect, was disregarded, although, when legitimate, and in unison with the design, Gluck, with the love of a pure artist, poured out his soul in such beauteous song as 'Che faro senza Eurydice.' The frequent interpellation of the chorus was likewise one of those happy conceptions of genius which mark the true reformer, and indeed the whole work is pervaded by that just proportion of strength and beauty which are the special characteristics of Attic art.

Some five years elapsed before Gluck again turned to the Greek tragedian for the choice of a subject. Enjoying the collaboration of Calzabigi, who had arranged the libretto for 'Orpheus,' the artist and the poet selected 'Alceste' for treatment. The principles which governed the art-creation of 'Orpheus' were carried into full effect in 'Alceste.' There was no endeavour or desire to temporize with the prevailing methods of Italian opera. Its supremacy was distinctly challenged, and at length overthrown by the mastery of Gluck's genius. We could have no better insight into the working of the artist's mind than that displayed in the dedicatory epistle addressed to the Duke of Tuscany. Speaking of the work he sought to accomplish, Gluck says : ' I seek to put music to its true purpose, that is, to support the poem, and thus to strengthen the expression of the feelings and the interest of the situation without interrupting the action ;' and, proceeding, he declares war against all those bad habits which had interrupted the unity of dramatic presentation.

Still imbued with his great art mission, 'Paris and Helen' appeared in 1770; but by this time the Viennese had had somewhat too much of the strong wine of genius. Their taste revived for a simple draught of sensuous melody, and Gluck, feeling the appreciation unequal to his merit, turned his eyes to Paris, where was preparing the greatest tragedy in modern history. Electric currents of intellectual emotion were flowing at this period between Paris and Vienna; and, even had there been no Corneille or Racine, no Lully or Rameau, the artistic sensitiveness of Gluck must have felt these currents of emotion generated by the intellects which were engaged in deadly struggle with the forms of tyranny and lust which enslaved and debased the manhood and womanhood of France. But there had been a Corneille and Racine, also a Lully and Rameau. What more natural, what more fitting, than that the artist who was to cement in some measure the labours of his brother poets and artists should feel his true home in such congenial atmosphere, and long to mingle the serenity and passion of his song with Corneille's majestic utterance and Racine's sympathetic adoration?

Turning to the latter poet, and generously assisted by Bailly du Rollet, with whom Gluck was in consultation, it was decided that 'Iphigénie en Aulide' should be selected to appeal to the

Parisians for their support of the new art principles. It was far from easy, however, to gain a hearing. Direct negotiations with the Grand Opera administration came to nothing, and they were at length prevailed on to grant a performance only through the combined influence of Maria Theresa, Empress of Austria, her son, the King of Rome, and her daughter, the Dauphine, Marie Antoinette. The occasion of the first performance was on April 19, 1774, and the work at once accentuated the differences which had arisen between Gluck and the adherents of the Italian school. The latter determined that supremacy should not be wrested from them without a severe struggle, and Piccini was put forward to champion their cause. The contest divided the musical populace of Paris, but Italian opera was doomed. A new spirit was abroad, a mighty spirit, which determined that, of all things, conventionality should be the least suffered. 'Iphigénie en Tauride' dealt a mortal stroke to the Piccini faction, and Gluck, in the realm of opera, was acknowledged supreme.

Amongst the partizans of Gluck was Rousseau. Voltaire likewise felt the fascination of his genius. These two men, dividing between them the intellectual sympathies of France, were engaged in a heroic attempt to rescue their country from falseness and conventionality. The days of Corneille and Racine had long since passed away with that brilliant intellectual assemblage which graced the administration of the great King. The men and women of France had fallen from their high estate. A polished sensuality, a habitual cynicism, decay of natural affection, a supreme arrogance founded upon caste, destructive of human sympathy, had destroyed virility and morals. Love was a mockery, and marriage a folly if the outcome of love; children, a necessary consequence to secure a title, but parental affection had vanished. The dignitaries of the Church had raised apostasy to a fine art. The people were the sport of the aristocratic classes.

But behold! the air is rent with lightning satire, and the righteous scorn of Voltaire scorches where it falls. Behold, too, Justice is preparing her scales, and from the calm and philosophic Montesquieu issues the spirit of the laws. And then a voice, the cry of a tortured spirit—a spirit that has been communing with itself. By intuition it has cleaved the heaven of ideality, by sad experience it has sounded hell's depths of sensuality. The voice is that of Rousseau. He has a message to deliver—the gospel of communion with one's self and nature. His 'Émile' stirs the breast of womanhood once more. The fountains of the great deep are opened, and the heart of France beats again in response to the appeal of natural love. But what of this? What has this moral reformation to do with Gluck? The creations of genius are the same yesterday, to-day, and for ever: for are they not part of the Word of God immortal, so far as they respond to those eternal laws of sympathy implanted in the human breast? Could Euripides have imagined when he saw the vision of Iphigénie clad in spotless purity of maiden innocence, and upon whom there was, as a halo, already set a crown of incomparable dignity—the majesty of noblest womanhood—that his imperishable ideal should help quicken into life that native admiration of virtue and sacrifice which, for the moment, seemed eclipsed in the heart of a great nation? Could Racine have imagined, as his genius commingled with the Greek, that the German should one day, by the passion and power of his art, invest with new beauty that sublime poem of resignation and sacrifice, qualities so essential to shape aright his country's destinies? Surely not; but this we know, that in those years directly anterior to the French Revolution, so pregnant with new forces to reshape the modern world, the art which expresses as none other the emotion of passion and desire allied itself in close communion with the high ideal of love and submissiveness unto death, and to the apostles and prophets of the new era lent the magic of its utterance and the beauty of its song.

Thus for ever genius is absolute—Euripides, Racine, Gluck, a trio of poets and musicians, linking the ages by spiritual communion and everlasting song.

In these two works, 'Iphigénie en Aulide' and 'Iphigénie en Tauride,' Gluck arrives at his full expression. At length, after many years of deep reflection, he has succeeded in realizing his conception of the mission of dramatic music, a conception which with intuitive sympathy transcribed the manifold emotions of man's nature in the language of the tonal art. His genius has in it the quality of universality, making him the peer and companion of the great artists and teachers. Divining the majesty of Hellenic utterance, he portrayed those lofty types of beauty which are the ages' priceless heritage. He shows us that virtue is not comparative but absolute; that, according to the gift of the spirit, one age differeth from another in glory, but each has its peculiar revelation. Could any artist do more? In a country which had well-nigh lost its lofty chivalrous instinct, where virtue was the paradise of fools, he taught in his art the inviolable majesty of womanhood and the sanctity of love.

Full of years and honours, he passed away on November 15, 1787, bequeathing to the greatest dramatic composer of this century, Richard Wagner, the mantle of his inspiration. Such vitality of principle is the worthiest monument of genius.

XXVI.

HAYDN.

WE have already passed in review three of those great tone masters who severally carried their art, in the domain applicable to their genius, to supreme perfection. The lyric, the epic, and the dramatic are personified for us in the names of Bach, Handel, and Gluck. Each brought to his time and place of working a lofty heroic ideal, each had a great message to deliver. Their types of humanity were drawn from long-gone ages; the past and the present were united by the sympathy of their genius.

In Joseph Haydn we have a mind of a different order—a mind typical of the great change to be wrought, and being wrought, in the thought of Europe. He is the poet of the present. The people's joys are his joys. He delights in their abandonment to simple pleasures; their songs and dance are to him a source of inspiration. His art work is coloured with this affection for the people. His association with them in early life, the comprehension of their needs, and of the cheerful spirit which relieved and animated their necessities, gave to his independent nature a genial and harmonious tone, a spontaneous and ofttimes ironical gaiety leavened with the leaven of the love of common humanity.

By his versatile qualities he was aptly fitted to become the mediator between the great masters who preceded him and those immortal tone poets, Mozart and Beethoven, who, in the catholicity of their genius, summed up the aspirations of an epoch, and left an imperishable ideal to light, with the beauty of its love and purity, the generations yet unborn.

Franz Joseph Haydn, better known as Joseph Haydn, the second son of Mathias Haydn, was born at Rohrau, a village in Lower Austria, on the night of March 31, 1732. His father's relatives on the male side were wheelwrights, and resided at Hainburg, a town on the Danube about four leagues distant from Rohrau. Here resided also a connection by marriage, one named Frankh, schoolmaster and chorregent, to whom presently little Haydn's education should be entrusted. Mathias himself was a wheelwright, and after the labours of the day would solace his evening leisure by playing upon the harp, and in singing to its accompaniment either by himself or with his wife. He doubtless had a sincere love for simple melody, and this love descended pre-eminently to Joseph, and in a less degree to his younger brother Michael. Little Joseph evinced keen interest in this evening music, while the performances of the village schoolmaster upon the violin were his wonder and delight. His father observed and encouraged these tendencies, and on one occasion when Frankh was visiting Rohrau embraced the opportunity to ask his opinion concerning Joseph's musical capacities. The result was that Frankh offered to superintend the lad's education, and thus it befell that Joseph, at the mature age of six, left his mother's side for ever at the call of the genius that was in him.

Frankh proved himself an able though harsh instructor. He had charge of his cousin for about two years when George Reutter, capellmeister of St. Stephen's Cathedral, Vienna, chanced to pay, amongst other places, a visit to Hainburg in search of voices for reinforcement of the Cathedral choir. Hearing from Frankh of Joseph's abilities, he decided to test them, and the result was so satisfactory that he offered to enroll the little chorister in the cantorei of St. Stephen's.

Mathias Haydn willingly consented to this brilliant future for his son, and when Joseph had completed his eighth year he entered the cantorei, which became his home until eighteen years of age. The years spent there were naturally very important. His early love of music became intensified. He enjoyed, it is true, no direct help from Von Reutter, but he cared little. Thrown on his own resources, he sought aid wherever it could be found, and, appealing to his father for assistance, he was rewarded with six florins, which he immediately expended in Fux's 'Gradus ad Parnassum' and Mattheson's 'Vollkommener Capellmeister.' With these companions he educated his genius, and sought to understand the principles of composition. Great misfortune, however, was in store for him. His brother Michael had also been admitted to the cantorei, and, Joseph's voice breaking, Michael, at the request of the Empress, took his place. Von Reutter sought now only a pretext to discharge him, and, a boyish freak furnishing the desired opportunity, he caned him as a parting blessing, and turned him, destitute and well-nigh broken-hearted, into the streets of Vienna on a dreary November evening in the year 1749. Poor and unbefriended, Haydn obtained no rest during that weary night. Morning found him still comfortless, roaming the Vienna streets. Sad and bitter must have been his thoughts, but genius sustained him, both now and during the months that were to follow.

Thus wandering, he met one Spangler, a tenor singer at the Church of St. Michael, who, with generous pity, conducted him to his own miserable garret, where he resided with his wife and child. This was Haydn's home during the winter months. A living had to be obtained by chance performances, by arrangement of compositions, and giving ill-paid lessons. At this dark hour a tradesman of Vienna, Buchholz, lent him unconditionally one hundred and fifty florins. It was a generous gift, and one gratefully requited and never forgotten. From that moment, although very poor, the clouds of adversity lifted, and the sunshine of hope lighted Haydn's heart. He now removed to the Michaelerhaus, and rented an old garret. His clavier and the books already mentioned were still his beloved companions, but his merit was not long to remain unknown. On the third story of the Michaelerhaus resided the most renowned librettist of the day—the Italian poet Metastasio. He became acquainted with the young musician, and, feeling kindred sympathy with genius, introduced him eventually to Porpora, and entrusted him with the musical education of his favourite pupil Marianne Martinez.

Haydn now came under the influence of Emmanuel Bach. He had, out of his scanty savings, purchased the first six sonatas of this master, and upon the principles and methods of Bach's compositions he based much of his after life-work in the symphony, sonata, and quartet.

Bach's advice in his treatise on the right method of playing the clavier sank deeply into Haydn's mind. Melody, rather than pedantic adherence to traditional forms, was advocated, and accorded admirably with the gay, loving nature of Haydn's character. Haydn's engagement as the master of Marianne was likewise full of importance. It brought him into close contact with Porpora, who after his fashion imparted to him promiscuous information, and was also the means of his becoming the accompanist to the mistress of the Venetian Ambassador, Correr. The visit of the Ambassador to the baths at Mannersdorf resulted in Haydn's acquaintance with Gluck and other well-known musicians. We can well imagine how congenial this atmosphere of genius must have been, how refreshing to the spirit the gentle beauty of country life.

On returning to Vienna Haydn devoted himself with great ardour to study. Gradually the recognition of his talent widened. He gathered round him sympathetic friends. Amongst these was Baron Von Fürnberg, for whom Haydn wrote several string trios, and sherzandi for wind instruments, the precursors of his symphonies and his first quartet. His genius at this time likewise gained for him the friendship of the accomplished Countess Von Thun. It was her influence, combined with that of Baron Von Fürnberg, which procured for Haydn the capellmeistership to Count Morzin, who resided at Lukavec, near Pilsen. For the orchestra he now found at his command he wrote several divertimenti for wind and strings, and other compositions, including his first symphony, which, though very slight, foreshadowed in clearness of expression and unity of design the characteristics which will ever remain associated with the name of the master.

It was at this period that Haydn married. He had conceived an ardent affection for one of his pupils, the younger daughter of a hairdresser named Keller, but her determination to enter a cloister frustrated his hope of happiness. Unfortunately, however, he was induced to marry her elder sister, Maria Anna. The union proved to be thoroughly unhappy, and eventually ended in a formal separation.

An event now took place which was to relieve Haydn from the worries of a perpetual struggle for subsistence. Count Morzin found himself compelled to disperse his orchestra, and using his influence for Haydn, he induced Prince Paul Anton Esterhazy to engage him as Vice-Capellmeister. It was, however, some months before he received the appointment, but his entry into the Esterhazy service, the intelligent interest of his patron in music, the means which were placed at his disposal to perfect the orchestra, were precisely those factors which were a heaven-sent boon to a musician who was destined to solidify and crystallize the forms of the symphony, sonata, and quartet, Haydn's special art mission.

It is not our intention to follow precisely the details of Haydn's life. We have seen how valiantly he surmounted the obstacles imposed by poverty; how the constant aspirations of his genius induced the study which gave him the mastery over diverse forms of musical expression, so that, the opportunity presenting itself, he was prepared to mould into organic unity those various forces which were seeking a perfect and abstract expression in the tonal art. Haydn's claim to be the father of modern instrumentation is based upon this capacity—not the invention, but the gathering up of the various elements, their direction and solidification by the exercise of an intuitive perception of balance and proportion, through which the related parts form a perfect whole. To understand this it will be necessary to trace briefly the evolution of the sonata and the symphony.

The sonata, as its name implies, is purely a sound-piece, but this gives little, if any, indication of the various elements which were in due time resolved and ordered into definite forms contrasting one with the other, and yet in their entirety presenting an organic unity which should be the perfect expression in lucidity and concentration of the composer's thought. It is of great interest to note the influences which were working to render possible this triumph in art manifested both in the beauty and strength of form, and in the presentment of a lofty ideal. The name sonata appears to have been adopted in contrast to that of cantata. Its origin really lay in a keen yearning to obtain a symmetrical expression in sound which should satisfy the more emotional æsthetic instincts generated by the mental forces of the Renaissance. The majesty of polyphonic utterance was representative of the highest achievements of the mediæval spirit, submission of the individual to authority; the new expression was *par excellence* of the individual, the searching for the hidden things of the spirit. The culmination of the sonata form in Beethoven compared in time with and was the outcome of the same circumstances which moulded the great individual intellects of Europe.

The madrigal and the dance were the primary constituent elements from which evolved an art form capable of embodying the most severely abstract and ideal conceptions. The accompaniment of the voice parts of the madrigal with viols led to the conception of a vague form of instrumental music which gave birth to the instrumental canzona, while the old order of dance tunes, known under various designations by the distinct order of their rhythmic motions, supplemented by ideas borrowed from the instrumental preludes and vocal portions of the drama, supplied a rough basis of form leading to the definite lines of structure in the modern sonata. Ecclesiastical influence was sometimes apparent, as in the first movements of the earliest sonatas. In those, for instance, written by Biber and Kuhnau there are several fugal movements, but the latter writer in his endeavour to balance defined and distinct subjects, and 'to distribute key and subject in large expanses,' felt clearly the intellectual craving for form which was soon to be so perfectly satisfied.

Corelli, the gifted violinist, exercised a great influence over the development of sonata form.

Alike in those written for Church and chamber, he was generally in favour of four movements, and strove to impart to them a certain amount of balance by variation of their time character. To quote from the exhaustive article in Grove's 'Dictionary of Music and Musicians,' to which I am greatly indebted, the first movement is commonly in 4-time of dignified and solid character. The second in the Church sonata is freely fugal, but in the chamber sonata variable, being in some an Allemande, in others a Courante. The third movement, in a different key from the first and last, is generally characteristic as being one in which composers endeavoured to incorporate a vague and tender sentiment, while the last movement is invariably of a lively character.

Corelli had no definite principles of structure. He naturally hesitated to import into high-class music the formal time elements which alone existed in song and dance music; while as to form in those movements which are not fugal, he repeats the opening bars in another position in the scale, thus striving to convey an assurance, simple though it be, of balance. Another of his devices, found likewise in contemporary and succeeding composers, is that of 'repeating the concluding passage of the first half at the end of the whole, or of the concluding passages of one half, or both consecutively'; and we may accept this device in its gradual extension as the 'direct origin of the characteristic second section and second subject of modern sonata movements.'

In Corelli's pupils we have an advance to realization of modern sonata form. To quote again from Grove, they began to perceive 'the effect and significance of relations between chords and distinct keys, and consequent appearance of regularity of purpose in the distribution of both, and increased freedom of modulation.' This understood, in conjunction with the expansion 'of the opening passage into a first subject, the figures of the cadence into a second subject,' an advance was made to binary form, and the form of sonata thus became stereotyped until Haydn's day.

J. S. Bach, in his fourteen sonatas for the violin and clavier, formulated no new principles, but he availed himself of the slow movement to express the lofty and emotional qualities of his genius, and, although his methods of working were founded on the contrapuntal writers of the past, he showed how perfect a vehicle the sonata would become for expression of the noblest and deepest thoughts when a form should be found in harmony with the modern spirit.

In Domenico Scarlatti we come to a writer full of genial simplicity. In his sonatas for the harpsichord he discarded fugal principles, stating and restating his ideas with persistent clearness and identity in the same movement. This studied design imparts to his sonatas a clear and adequate structural effect, which goes far to satisfy the modern desire for form.

In the sonatas for the clavier at this period the order of movements was uncertain, but the internal structure increasingly manifested progress to clear binary form. This evolution is carried on through Hassé, Galuppi, Dr. Arne, and last, but not least, the brothers Wilhelm Friedemann and Carl Philip Emmanuel Bach. The impetus which Carl Philip gave to the study of the clavier was very great. His comprehension of its capacity and adaptability for certain forms of expression, allied with a clear method of working, gave him a considerable influence over the development of sonata form.

Thus, when Haydn appeared he became the inheritor of those tentative efforts which generations of musicians had made towards attaining an adequate, concise, and ordered expression of abstract feeling and devotion. Emmanuel Bach was his great teacher, and his influence is seen throughout the whole range of Haydn's instrumental compositions. In fact, as has been said, it was not the sonata but sonata form which became so important to Haydn.

With regard to the symphony, we find the term first applied to any portion of instrumental music whatever which might be considered an appendage to the vocal parts. These vocal parts were by far the most important, the instrumental portions being thrown in as a relief. In Peri's 'Eurydice,' a sinfonia occurs for three flutes, and very quickly the symphony became a most important element in dramatic works. At first the term seems to have been used indiscriminately.

The introduction to airs, recitatives, and even the instrumental portion of airs, when played by a single performer, were called symphonies; but by degrees the symphony became the introductory movement to the opera, and the initial step in its development was the endeavour to attain a certain mode of form.

Thus Lully sought to attain form by the balance of short divisions. The first movement would be slow and solid, the following lighter and quicker, and then again a slow movement, though not so grave in character as the first. This model, which became highly appreciated, was improved upon by Scarlatti, both in style and form; but the modern symphony is built upon the Italian overture. In this model the first and third movements are quick, and the intervening one slow, and such was the favour which this form attained that by the middle of the eighteenth century it was universally accepted.

The form thus attained, the development of internal structure naturally followed. Thus, early in the eighteenth century, the strings which had been almost solely employed by Lully and Scarlatti were reinforced by a large body of wind instruments, and though these were seldom employed all together, yet they were a source of strength, and produced 'contrasting degrees of full sound, if not contrasts of colour and of tone.' The internal development of the symphony seems to have closely followed that of its allied form, the sonata, so that it is difficult to decide in which the important detail first appeared of 'defining first and second principal sections by subjects decisively distinct.'

The indifference with which the symphony was first received when introduced to the opera induced composers to reserve their best efforts for the concert-room; and in consequence this form became one of the most favoured for chamber-music. The works of Stamitz, Emmanuel Bach, Christian Bach, and Abel, illustrate the development of instrumentation and definition of form. Gradually the various instruments assumed independence, and extreme regularity marked the general outlines of the symphony. 'The first movement was a vigorous broad allegro, the second a sentimental slow movement, the third a lively vivace.'

Previous to Haydn the great master of instrumentation was Emmanuel Bach, and Haydn was not slow to acknowledge his indebtedness, although his influence was derived primarily through the clavier sonata.

Having thus cursorily glanced at the evolution of the symphony and sonata, we see that the title claimed for Haydn as the father of modern instrumentation does not rest upon the invention of the forms mentioned, but rather upon that ever-growing appreciation of their character which led him to ennoble them and bring them into harmony with the new spirit of things. His consummate mastery of technical expression, his delight in symmetry and proportion, his polished and refined utterance, were the final outcome of many years of laborious study, and the well-nigh unequalled opportunities he enjoyed as Capellmeister at Eisenstadt and Esterhaz. The orchestra was ever at his command, and the conditions of his service encouraged him to renewed efforts.

Gradually the range of his vision widened; his artistic faculties were ever striving to reach an expression which should be at once both logical and beautiful. But though this was so, his genius was to be immensely quickened by contact with that of Mozart, and the generous appreciation which awaited him upon his arrival in England. The rapid maturity of Mozart's powers enabled the pupil ultimately to become the teacher of the master; but this detracts nowise from the genius of Haydn. His had been the labour, the continuous effort, to mould the forms bequeathed to him in the true symphonic fashion; and Mozart and Beethoven, not having to undergo this ordeal, could advance unimpeded upon the results thus obtained.

The relations of Haydn and Mozart were like those of father to son. In Haydn's genial and simple nature no room for jealousy could be found save that for the honour of his art. Again and again he testified to the inimitable genius of the young composer, and a bitter cry of anguish escaped him when he knew that he should see his face no more.

The visit to England, on which we need not dwell, marked an epoch in Haydn's life. Hitherto he had, as it were, been constantly assimilating and experimenting. The long course of effort had moulded the art form of the symphony, sonata, and quartet, and now the time of freedom had come.

If the symphony and sonata were, as we have seen, so indebted to the formative qualities of Haydn's genius, much more so was it with the quartet. His first essay, simple as it is, contains those art forms which came to such glorious fruition in the quartets of Beethoven and Schumann; but throughout the quartets written by Haydn there can be traced an advance in richness of thought and mastery of part-writing, until he had elaborated this form of composition into a perfect vehicle of refined and sympathetic utterance.

Such, then, was the character of Haydn's genius, a genius self-directed, enjoying only the guidance, the indications of certain art forms, found in the works of his predecessors, which, however, he elaborated by his perception and intuition into the noblest forms of instrumental music.

It remains for us to mention Haydn's efforts in oratorio. While in London he had listened to the majestic rendering of Handel's 'Messiah,' and Salomon incited him to efforts in a similar direction. The outcome was the 'Creation,' and subsequently the 'Seasons.' The simple and pure character of Haydn found expression in the former, and each morning and evening he prayed for enlightenment. Although oratorio was not the fitting music for the display of Haydn's powers, the 'Creation' had a brilliant and worthy success. Pearls of incomparable melody abound, and honours fell thick and fast upon the master. The 'Seasons' met with similar approbation, but the effort cost Haydn his imaginative power. No great work flowed from his pen thereafter; his efforts and labours were now drawing to a close.

Haydn's last days were spent in seclusion, and pervaded by a peaceful melancholy. Once only was the calm broken. The Society of Amateurs in Venice, on March 27, 1808, gave a performance of the 'Creation,' at which Haydn was enabled for a short time to be present. The venerable master was seated by the side of the Princess Esterhazy, and Salieri conducted. The enthusiasm was unbounded; but Haydn, with simple pathos, acknowledged as the source of his genius the Father of Light. The emotion of the master, however, became so great that it was thought advisable for him to leave at the close of the first part. His beloved friends and pupils gathered round him, and amongst them Beethoven, upon whom was to fall the mantle of his inspiration, and who was to carry to such glorious perfection the forms bequeathed to him.

XXVII.

MOZART.

AMONGST the greatly gifted of mankind there are a few whose names suggest the sunshine and the joy of life—not because sorrow has forborne to mingle its shadow with the light of genius, but because that genius is so grand and pure, so reflective of the refined beauties of existence, that in its presence we feel a joy and innocence incompatible with mental strife, and productive only of deep peace. Such are the feelings interwoven with the memory of Mozart, that incomparable tonal poet, whose works have conferred upon humanity incalculable joy, lightening its burden with the sympathy of universal beauty.

Such men seem to belong to no nation. Plato, Shakespeare, Raphael, Mozart — mankind, with loving emulation, seeks but to honour them, to write their names among the first of the immortals.

But, though this is so, yet their genius is none the less the product of the idiosyncrasy of their national individuality. They came to the birth through the manifold influences of their time. Their work, indeed, is but the consummation of those influences wrought in passionate effort of fulfilment into imperishable beauty, both of form and expression.

At the time of Mozart's birth his star, indeed, was a bright one, amid the constellation of genius. Lessing and Winckelmann, Goethe and Schiller, Gluck and Handel, Kant and Fichte, indicate the wide range of German thought, its moral grandeur, its perception of the beautiful, its invincible patriotism. Slowly and surely the lines were being laid by which the intellectual supremacy in Europe passed to Germany, by which, too, its supremacy in arms should be attested.

Of the grace and sensibility of German genius no two more distinguished names could be mentioned than Goethe and Mozart. Of prophetic and impassioned utterance, of the weaving of sorrow and of joy, of human agitation with the calm serenity of sustained spirituality, the great seer and poet was to come in Beethoven. How came it, then, that Germany at this period should be so rich in minds of such diverse orders, that all at once should burst upon the vision this galaxy of genius, philosophy, and art?

The influences had been preparing since the close of the Thirty Years' War. At the termination of that drear and exhaustive struggle the German nation found itself without any political coherence. Men of talent, debarred from active personal participation in politics, sought for their reviving energies the more glorious career of letters. Literary unions were founded, multiplied, and flourished. The German language was pruned and cultivated, and, mid the retirement of the various courts, that equable temperament of life prevailed so admirably adapted and even provocative to reflective growth.

It needed but the stimulating influence of French and English thought for the German thinkers to become the keenest analysts in the mental laboratory of Europe, and ere long both natural and moral science were revolutionized as to methods and conceptions. The promise of German poetry, too, received more than ample fulfilment in Goethe and Schiller, while the deeply imaginative side of the German nature, its abstract metaphysical genius, was abundantly illustrated in a crowd of writers.

For art, music was the pleasure and solace of every court, and this fact is the cause of German ascendancy in music. Men of wealth and eminence vied with each other in their patronage of the art, and talent and genius were sure of recognition, if not of pecuniary recompense.

The Court at Salzburg was one of many similar which supported its trained musicians and orchestra. At the time of Mozart's birth his father, Leopold Mozart, was Court composer and conductor. In tracing the genealogy of the family, we find its early members endowed with artistic instincts, and these, in the case of Leopold Mozart, were so strong that he abandoned the study of jurisprudence for the pursuit of music. Leopold Mozart was indeed a notable man, of strong intelligence, penetrating judgment, and possessed of a thorough mastery of the technicalities of his art. Never has genius received more careful and loving instruction than that which père Mozart imparted to his divinely gifted son. He felt himself but the guardian of supreme gifts, and worthily did he labour to ensure the rich promise of their harvest.

Mozart was born on January 27, 1756. His mother was a Maria Anna Pertl, and both she and her husband were distinguished for their handsome personal appearance. A numerous family was the offspring of the marriage, but two children only survived — the renowned Mozart and his distinguished sister, Maria Anne.

It was while Leopold Mozart was fostering and educating the early talent for music displayed by his little daughter that Wolfgang's love and passion for music were manifested. Seated at the harpsichord, he would strike consecutive thirds, and endeavour to imitate the tunes played by his sister. His father observed these signs, and at once devoted himself to the musical education of his son. It became immediately apparent that a marvellous genius had been born, a genius so versatile, so universal in its sympathy, as to take equal rank among the great creative artists of all time. No story evolved from the imagination could surpass the narrative of the young child's achievements. In very truth it may be said that he was inspired with the spirit of harmony, and his instinct of due regard for form was only equalled by the grace and freedom manifested within its limits.

Of course, little Mozart enjoyed the constant superintendence of his father, but, as a mere child, his genius received homage in the principal cities of Europe—Vienna, Paris, London, Milan, Florence, Venice, Rome. The winsome grace of childhood always surrounded him. He would fling his arms in simple affection round the neck of an Empress, and constitute himself the companion of princes. Very charming is the picture of the Mozart family at this period—father, son, and daughter — as they travelled hither and thither, here received with *éclat* at Court, there enjoying the hospitality of some simple monks, repaying them with wonderful recitals upon the convent organ. But this picture has been so often drawn that we will pass on to consider the true significance of Mozart in the history of music.

Mozart's great characteristic was receptivity, allied with a genius which, as in the case of Shakespeare and Raphael, was able to assimilate all previous experience, and utilize it through an exquisite perception of the beautiful for the production of the choicest works. Like the two great masters with whom we have compared him, this receptivity is never allowed to assume the form of mere imitation. It was an imperious necessity for him to reproduce as far as might be those visions of abstract beauty which haunt every poet's soul, and to say in his peculiar way, and none other, the things which had been committed to him. But this peculiar way was full of light and grace, whose spell is so potent that there is a danger of disregarding the profound knowledge of the forms and technicalities of art, without which, however great the genius, no masterpiece could result.

On the one hand Mozart learned of and inspired Haydn, on the other he presaged those deeps of emotion laid bare by Beethoven. But everywhere and always he is Mozart. His is the gift of grace—that faculty divine by which the orb of his genius is luminous above all others. Occupying as he does the position of mediator between Haydn and Beethoven, yet he is the last of the great musicians who contents himself within the strict limits of his art. But his fertility within these limits, his clothing of dry forms with all the wealth and witchery of imagination, surpass in this direction the efforts of either of his great compeers. It was reserved for Beethoven to discover a new world in music, to break down the barriers between music and poetry; but the mastery of all that we understand by the name of form culminates in Mozart. He is one of the great examples in modern art of that genius that can attain perfection within prescribed limits. This intuitive appreciation of form disclosed itself in Mozart's earliest years, and it may be said he could assimilate form at will. Both with Haydn and Mozart it was a great factor. Through the genius of the former the efforts of previous composers had been wrought into consistent unity; and Mozart, learning of Haydn, was enabled, undiverted, to direct his great powers to the work of perfecting.

How great these powers, may be judged by his contribution to the development of the symphony and sonata. In the early years of his career he, like Haydn, wrote numerous symphonies which can only be regarded, comparatively, as exercises in facile expression. But the potentialities of instrumental music broke forcibly upon him at Mannheim. The excellence of the Mannheim orchestra was of wide renown, and its performances disclosed to Mozart the possibilities that lay hidden in the symphonic form. A great poet, he made it a vehicle for the most tender, passionate, and dignified emotions of our nature; a great artist, he employed the resources of colour, tonal combination and effect, to convey with adequate expression the burden of those emotions. Here, at least, that vision of perfect beauty which Mozart ever saw was translated in the pure medium of tonal language to aspiring though less gifted humanity, and a possession of beauty and joy for evermore committed to its keeping.

Moreover, the production of these symphonies had a great effect upon the similar compositions of Haydn. This master had been working with untiring effort to expand and enrich the forms bequeathed to him, but it was the illuminating genius of his friend and brother-artist that awoke all the possibilities of his music-loving nature, and the world was the richer by the magnificent symphonies which he produced for the Salamon concerts in London.

Mozart's contribution to the sonata was one of grace and delicacy of finish. Here, as in the symphony, he found the form well-nigh matured, but within that form the refinement of his genius was fully manifested. We in these later times find it difficult to realize the satisfaction which this formal perfection gave to Mozart's contemporaries, but this should not blind us to the great work which Mozart accomplished for the sonata. He further elaborated and crystallized the forms, making them lustrous with the pure radiance of exquisite grace and adornment.

But we only commence dimly to understand Mozart's genius when we contemplate his achievement in opera. To Gluck it had been given to prune the opera of its excrescences, and to present, with consistent unity, the action of the drama. But Mozart's intuitive perception gave to him all that Gluck had laboriously wrought for, while the sympathy of his genius enabled him to exhibit what to Gluck was ever denied, the humorous and the comic as well as the pathetic and austere side of human character. Upon the one hand, Mozart may be compared with Raphael in the exquisite grace, colouring, and harmony of his compositions, on the other he is allied to Shakespeare by the grandeur of his dramatic conception. The whole range of human emotion finds in him a sympathetic interpreter. He understands and illumines the varied elements of our nature. Like all great artists, he is indifferent as to whence he derives the sources of inspiration, but with them he is equally careful in selection. From the French and Italian methods he winnows the chaff by the breath of his genius and creates, in 'Don Giovanni,' the supreme masterpiece of romantic opera. His art is truly the vehicle of the world-spirit. Yet how indifferent he was to the manner in which he wrought, yet how patriotic, is evidenced by his opera 'Die Zauberflöte!' Indifferent in this sense only: he knew that his genius was independent of what was supposed to be the only vehicle for opera—the Italian—and he longed to justify his complaints against the meagre support granted to native effort. Like Lessing, Goethe, and Schiller, he wrought for the emancipation of his country's thought and expression from foreign domination, and in the 'Magic Flute' convincingly demonstrates that the language of genius is that which it deliberately adopts.

Although we have now indicated Mozart's great achievements in the symphony, sonata, and opera, yet this slight survey would be incomplete without mention of him as a Church composer. In his earliest years he naturally fell under the influence of his father, and the compositions of Michael Haydn were likewise much admired by him. His gift of sympathetic receptivity is nowhere more conspicuous than in this branch of art, and although we are unable to deal with the subject in detail, it is mentioned to introduce his last and crowning masterpiece, 'The Requiem.' The sorrowful premonition that he was writing this Mass to commemorate his approaching death was, alas! too true, and, as it were, conscious of that silent and unhonoured burial which even now fills our hearts with shame, his genius, seeking consolation in the glorious perfection of its power, and his soul that peace which only flows from the deeps of eternal love, rose to supreme effort in this supplicatory appeal for mercy and reconciliation. To Mozart, as to all minds of the first order, the titanic conflict between the opposing principles of good and evil was an absorbing consideration. The great mystery ever demanding solution can only find partial interpretation and utterance through the mind of genius, and if we have in 'Don Giovanni' metaphysical qualities in kind with Goethe, in 'The Requiem' the master has enshrined those consolations of the Christian faith to which alone the human mind, weary of speculation, turns at last for a solution of the mystery in love.

But although the shadow of death was lengthening, it served only to enhance the brilliancy of the master's faculties. Too late were now the offers of assistance and of release from the necessity of earning his daily bread by uncongenial occupation. Never has artist worked in an atmosphere of greater disillusionment than Mozart. Conscious of unequalled genius, it was repaid by a like neglect; and now, when he had arrived at maturity of expression, when he had at last absorbed all that the past could teach, from which, by the revivifying power of his genius, he was capable of producing new and immortal effects, death came, and his wealthy and admiring contemporaries accorded him a pauper's and an unknown grave.

In 'The Requiem' the essence of Mozart's genius is concentrated. Grandeur and liberality of conception, majestic dignity, vivid tonal colouring, and massing of orchestral combination, are welded by a serene grace into one of the most perfect expressions in the realm of religious art.

Thus worthily did the master close his career, a career ushered in with all the warmth and sunlight of genius, welcomed wherever the brilliancy of its rays penetrated, terminated amidst jealousy and intrigue, a weary struggle with poverty and ofttimes indifference. And then, when these seemed vanquished, and a rift appeared in the clouds of adversity, it was but to admit the messenger of death, to rescue one of the purest souls that dwelt amongst humanity, for Mozart's follies were as dust in the balance compared with his serene purity of conception and trust in that Eternal Love which he supplicated so beseechingly, and which assuredly admitted him to its presence for evermore.

XXVIII.

BEETHOVEN.

WHEN Mozart had passed the portal of death into immortality it must have seemed to many there was no one upon whom his mantle of inspiration could worthily fall. That beautiful soul momentarily eclipsed while mounting in meridional splendour, and from whom, as a parting gift, came outpouring that majestic song which chants the glory of the departed, seemed so lustrous in the firmament of genius, as to allow the light of no other star.

But the unity of German genius had yet to be completed—Bach, Handel, Haydn, Gluck, Mozart. Bach, that great high-priest whose works are the fount of law and inspiration; Handel, the epic singer of his race, weaving in glorious song of majesty and might the glories of the glorious; Gluck, the great artist, feeling the throb of human passion and the majesty of classic virtue; Haydn, that simple soul, who spoke in simple tones to his brother-men, making them kin by the humanity of his genius; Mozart, the sublime, to whom the world was a world of melody, and life, though full of pain, yet fuller still of hope, who translating, and translated, became the minister of grace and sweetest consolation, and then—a genius, the genius of his era, full of reverence and yet of revolution, reverence for all that was worthy and beautiful in life, impatient of everything fettering the just freedom of the soul, sweeping from before him with the storm-blast of genius all puerilities whatsoever, laughing to scorn the cherished laws of pedants, and from the deeps of earth and the pure height of heaven gathering the innate harmonies of law and divinest melody of love.

Yes, the old order giveth place to the new—that old order which, having long ceased to lead the people, made them at last their slaves; the new order riding upon the whirlwind of a nation's vengeance uncontrolled, the new order heralded by Voltaire and Rousseau, the French Revolution, panting for liberty, full of noble impulses, hurried into demoniac acts, whose strength, diverted by Napoleon for selfishness, gave Europe liberty by breaking down the barriers of geographical boundaries, and causing men to act together in unity against tyranny.

The supreme fact of the era, the Revolution, physical, political, spiritual, demanded a supreme artist. This artist was Beethoven, unconsciously if you will; but the universal sweep of his genius, his titanic power, his purity, his love, are the elements of the new life born with the new years of the present century. And with Beethoven Germany completed the circle of her tone poets —that Germany who found the prophet of the Reformation in Luther, found the poet of its sequel the Revolution in Beethoven, and the whole scope of her genius in those great artists we have mentioned, to find a parallel for whose achievements we must go back to the golden age of ancient Greece.

Let us see what manner of man this supreme artist was.

Born at Bonn, probably December 16, 1770, it was soon apparent that birth had dowered genius with poverty, and circumstances hedged around a native tenderness and imperial pride a well-nigh insuperable barrier. A mocking, cynical spirit seemed to have gone forth to meet Beethoven in the fastnesses of life, saying, 'This genius shall be your torture—submit. I will deprive thee of the choicest desires of thy being: the hope of an ideal love in womanhood, and delight in the innermost expression of nature's utterance.' But as a hero of heroes, the loss of one turned but his spirit in supplication to the Love Eternal, and deprivation of the other to that defiance of the external which before the concentred passion of his genius, and the ardent inspiration of his love, rolled away as a scroll, and made him for all time Nature's supreme poet. Yes, the time had come, and Germany, yea, Europe, in the birth-throes of that tempestuous thought-era had brought forth a man—the tone poet—who, as no other yet has done, has sounded the deeps of life, and by subtlest sympathy of interpretation disclosed the spiritual glories of the universe.

We need not linger long over the career of the child Beethoven. When yet but three years of age death removed his grandfather, one of his few, bright, and cherished memories, and left him but his mother for consolation. His father, rendered ofttimes incapable by intemperance, played the part of despotic instructor, and no greater contrast can be imagined between the parental solicitude and wise guidance which fostered the genius of Mozart than that bestowed upon his great contemporary and successor.

Tears and weariness, and that constitutional reserve which ever made Beethoven solitary, were a poor substitute for that delight which should wait on childhood; but time passes, and Beethoven gathers instruction from various sources, from Pfeiffer, the friend of his father, from one Zambona, a teacher of languages, from Van den Eeden, the old Court organist, and last, though not least, from Neefe his successor. He became, likewise, when twelve years of age, cymbalist in the orchestra, and thus early he learned the elements of art, which were afterwards to be welded into such perfect unity.

What nebulæ of glory, what divine shapes floated on the far horizon of the boy's imaginings, all those who have felt the quickening of creative power will assuredly understand; and how, when from Vienna (that Vienna rendered trebly illustrious as the residence of Gluck, Haydn, and Mozart) came on the breath of fame, the echo of immortal melody, or the far strain of triumphant acclaim, called forth by the splendour of some new achievement, we can see the kindling eye and hear the throbbing heart as there arises the irrepressible desire to go, reverence, and achieve.

And it was to be, though how we know not, for at this time stern want was the constant companion of the Beethovens; but through whatever unknown generosity, Beethoven, in the year ever memorable 1787, set forth to fulfil his cherished hope, and stand face to face with the great maestro of the day, Mozart. We can imagine the meeting. The young lad, conscious of none greater, standing in the presence of the known greatest; Mozart rather listless, perhaps unconsciously recalling the days of his youth, those golden days when before him lay the sunlit vista of immortal fame. And now the end is coming, and achievement—ah! what could he not achieve, what heavens lie open to his vision, what immortal strains are ringing in his ears, if these frivolous Viennese would, by keeping him from the dire necessity of want, free him for the high purpose of his destiny. The lad plays, and

Mozart, ever courteous, commends him. But young Beethoven knows that he has not touched the soul of the artist. No current of electric sympathy unites their spirits. But it must be. There is anguish in the thought were it not so. May he improvise? And now one soul appeals to the other, and they know and understand. And Mozart, perhaps still thinking, commends the youth to the care of these same Viennese, whose want of care was fretting away the life of one of the purest of God's sons.

But while in the full enjoyment of this visit Beethoven is suddenly recalled to Bonn. His mother is dying—she who is dearest to him of all on earth, who comprehends, as a mother alone can comprehend, his many vagaries and the passionate strivings of his genius—the desire to be anywhere save in that restricted circle, yet who never murmurs, but binds himself to her by chivalrous ties of love and noblest sense of duty, for in this same sense Beethoven was ever of the noblest. Listen to his words:

'So good, so amiable a mother, she was my best friend. Ah! who was happier than I, so long as I was able to utter the sweet name of mother, and to know that I was heard? And to whom can I now say it?—to the silent images of her that my imagination conjures up.'

And then, in the November of the same year, his little sister Margaretha also passed away. In the presence of this loss, and the increasing infirmities of his father, whatever high hopes had been called forth by his visit to Vienna seemed rudely dissipated.

The necessities of life demanded what was ever to him a most hateful task—that he should give lessons; but this sacrifice of inclination led to a rich recompense in the friendship which resulted with the Von Breunings. To the lad mourning the loss of his mother, and to whom, as to all genius, the refinement and grace of life were a refreshing stimulus to the creative faculty, this close, pure friendship was of inestimable worth. The discernment of Madame Von Breuning quickly discovered the strength and genius of the boy-teacher, reinforced as they were by the sterling quality of unfaltering rectitude, and even in his least controllable moments her graceful tact and laughing satire restored good humour and repose.

Franz Ries and Wegeler were also constant visitors at the house of the Von Breunings, while the daughter Eleanore and her brother Stephen, in spite of interruptions caused by Beethoven's irascible temperament, remained his devoted friends. Moreover, he partook here of that liberal culture provided for his pupils, and the genius of Lessing and Klopstock, Goethe and Shakespeare, Milton and Sterne, and the grand imagery of the 'Odyssey,' sank deep into congenial soil.

That there was something peculiarly attractive in the personality of Beethoven there can be no doubt, for at this time he formed yet another and close friendship with the amiable and gifted Count Waldstein, who so frequently gave valuable advice and encouragement, and also smoothed away with rare delicacy of tact many a pecuniary difficulty. Through the instrumentality of the latter many a noble house lay open to Beethoven when he presently left Bonn for Vienna, and we may be quite sure he lost no opportunity of influencing the Elector in favour of his young protégé.

Thus a few years passed away, his father being the one great anxiety, and whose incapacity became such as to render it necessary for his son to assume the guardianship of the family. But all was now drawing to a close. The visits of Haydn to Bonn, both in 1790 and in 1792, on his journeys to and from London, doubtless revived all the old longing, the intense desire for action and achievement. Vienna was the lodestar, and with a small pension from the Elector, and with the aid and encouragement of his friends, especially of Waldstein, who, with prophetic instinct, discerned in him Mozart's successor, the young musician left his native place in November, 1792.

Well-nigh immediately he placed himself under the tuition of Haydn, but the calm, genial spirit of the old man never apparently gauged the tempestuous intensity of his pupil's nature. Perhaps, as he surveyed him, he thought a little nonchalant treatment, which a man of the world knows so well how to deal to those whom he regards as overweening and presumptuous, would do Beethoven's rough and assertive nature no harm; but be this as it may, no two natures were further sundered save in the common love and honour of their art. We can picture to ourselves the young and imperious musician. Nursed in the comparative solitude of Bonn, already imagining as his by right the fame of Mozart and the renown of Haydn, conscious of gifts and power which rendered him even scornful of those who had attained fame while yet himself almost unknown, treating the conventionalities of polite life in Vienna with a contumely and contempt, which scarce savoured of consideration, it was small wonder that Haydn nicknamed him the Great Mogul, and that Albrechtsberger, in holy horror, should gasp at his presumption.

But we know now, what they could not, that these manifestations of independence were but the assertion of a unique genius, a genius which, while studying law, and endeavouring to express itself by law, would yet guard itself with reverence from any limitations which would stay the sweep of its power and the interpretation of its expression.

The presence of Beethoven, too, in the drawing-rooms of Vienna must have been very refreshing, and prayers and entreaties were alike unavailing, if he were unwilling, to move him from his purpose, and no rank whatever stayed the torrent of his invective if he felt himself aggrieved. Altogether the young musician must have been a rare acquisition in Viennese circles.

Of the poets and artists which the modern world has as yet brought forth, there stand out three of supreme import. Stamped on the visage of each are the records of that journey through the abodes of woe, swept by the fire and tempest of passion, and watered by the waters of an agonizing grief—Dante, Michael Angelo, and Beethoven. The unrest of their being drove them into the deep abyss; the inconvertible purity of their nature bore them into sunlit regions of eternal calm. But between these two extremes they alternated, and their poetry and their art interpret for us the universal life.

The visage of Beethoven is his truest history. Defiance, scorn, indomitable pride, the lightning-play of genius; the deep abstraction in which the spirit has escaped from the clothing of the material into the immaterial, with its realities and verities, its decrees of fate and unfolding of wisdom, mingled with a giant power of intellect and a vast sympathy, without which all other gifts whatsoever would have been of no avail to have interpreted the Divine message which he bequeathed—all these qualities are envisaged in the great artist.

As a young man, then, we can well understand how Beethoven appeared to his contemporaries. How Czerny saw in him, clothed in garments of some long-haired texture, a facetious resemblance to Robinson Crusoe; how others, as they broke in upon his solitude, found his rooms in confusion indescribable, remnants of food, scattered furniture, the littering of manuscripts, and the master, half dressed, and that recklessly, oblivious of all things earthly, moulding into some glorious work of art the Divine ideas for which he waited so patiently and laboured so laboriously.

Beethoven is the great hero of modern art. Around him were men the most illustrious. Napoleon was scattering the nations, and in the first burst of that defiance of the old *régime* which France, in her enthusiasm for the sublime idea of fraternity, flung down as battle-gage to Europe, Beethoven, the poet and the prophet of the new era, thinking he discerned the saviour of society, composed his splendid 'Eroica' symphony, and dedicated it to the prowess of Buonaparte. But his idol had but feet of clay, and with righteous rage and scorn he tore into fragments the name of the founder of the new tyranny and a base imperialism. To Goethe, who could from the Weimarian range of culture view with a speculative interest and calm curiosity the progress of the European whirlwind, and who, in youth and age, delighted himself with sentimental amours, Beethoven shows by contrast as fire to fireworks. His love was indeed a passion, but it was a passion of such ideal purity that it sought alliance with those who, from their very station, were precluded from accepting it; but, failing this, never did it unfold its pinions in lesser flight, or seek delight in sensual love. How grim, too, was his raillery of the poet when the latter uncovered himself obsequiously before some royal insipidities; how careless of the salutations which, in reality given to him, were appropriated with such fond conceit by Goethe! Yes! these trivialities had no delight as such to Beethoven, although he could vindicate himself with more than success against those who assailed his dignity. But, if we see him thus on the assertive side of his character, we also know how tender and affectionate he was. His love for his mother, his patience with the infirmities of his father, his forbearance with his brothers, and that great love for his unworthy nephew which brought him down with bitter grief to death, besides those close and loving friendships which, when imperilled by his harsh and hasty words, gave him such remorseful concern, all testify to the complexities of a nature full as it were of impatient contradictions.

But there was a friend to whom throughout his life he laid bare the recesses of his being, and from whom he ever gathered inspiration, repose, and love, a friend who could meet him in every mood—in the violence of the tempest, in the depth of calm, in the radiance of the sunlight, in the deepening of the shade, in joyous raillery and in solemnity of tone—she alone who could respond to his inmost call, and draw together in loving unity the elements of his being—Nature. What deprivation, then, what infliction, what agony of uncontrollable desire, swept over his desolated being when the voice of her, his only and beloved mistress, reached his ears no more, it is impossible to understand. Cruel fate! but perhaps how merciful to his deepest genius was the infliction which caused the loss to him, more precious than aught else, of the sense of hearing. As Milton translated his grief into the lament of Samson, and Handel poured forth his lamentation in his incomparable setting of the poet's words, so Beethoven, in the mid-day of manhood, tortured with the fading possibility of recovery, bade good-bye to hope and Nature's intercourse. Hear what he says: 'Even the cherished hope which I brought here with me of being cured, at least to a certain extent, has now utterly forsaken me; it has faded like the fallen leaves of autumn. Almost as I came here, so do I depart. Even the lofty hope that upheld me during the beautiful summer days has vanished. Oh, Providence! let one more day of pure joy be vouchsafed to me! The echo of true happiness has so long been a stranger to my heart. When, when, O God, shall I again be able to feel it in the temple of nature and of man? Never—no! oh, that were too hard!'

But the heroic spirit is unquenched: 'Patience! I must now choose her for my guide. This I have done. I hope to remain firm in my resolve until it shall please the relentless Fates to cut the thread of life. Perhaps I shall get better, perhaps not. I am prepared. To have to turn philosopher in my twenty-eighth year is no easy task, harder for the artist than for anyone else. Oh, God! Thou lookest down upon my inmost soul. Thou knowest, Thou seest, that love to my fellow-men and all kindly feelings have their abode there.'

Thus, then, we come to an event which must have had the greatest influence upon the character of Beethoven's genius—an influence which in all probability was not evil, but good, and which, by the merciful law of compensation, drove him of necessity into the deeps of feeling, and resulted, if not in the most perfect, at least in as perfect works of art, as the genius of man has ever given as offerings to his fellows. Let us see whether we can obtain a glimpse of the evolving and characteristics of this genius.

The chief characteristics of Beethoven's early youth and manhood were reflective intensity and a noble purpose in his art. From the outset of his career we find no desire to merely please; his one unfaltering wish was supreme excellence. The wide range of his thought, the sweep of his power, combined with that which we only find in the greatest of masters, intensity of perception into the cardinal principles of things, precluded him from any prolific output in the early days of his career. The union of these qualities made him dissatisfied with every living master. Neither Haydn nor Mozart satisfied him. Not content with the theoretical canons of Albrechtsberger, his audacity had to be repaid from experience. But still the living principle of his genius was dissatisfaction, and, grasping the spiritual, he found the means of ultimate attainment. All his great works grew up organically—first the seed, the idea, dropped into the congenial soil of allied thought, whose fertilizing qualities supplied the nutritive power and accumulative strength whereby the idea, expanding under the efforts of incessant culture, and pruned of all excrescences, blossomed at last into the flower and fruit of art. Thus those wonderful symphonies grew up: most wonderful of all that ninth symphony, wherein, if ever man has shown himself poet, priest, and king, unfolding, revering, and controlling the forces of emotion displayed in nature and in man, he has done so here. In the realm of art and intellect no greater achievement exists. As Beethoven matured we note the access of strength. We have seen under what obligations we lay to Haydn and Mozart in building up the form of the sonata and symphony. The inestimable gift which these masters gave us was the form; the inestimable worth of what Beethoven gave to us was the transcription of life born with the opening years of this century. Mozart, as it were, bridged the interval from the eighteenth to the nineteenth century. Beethoven crossed the bridge and interpreted for us with prophetic insight the new life. Courtly life was dead. The French Revolution and Napoleon, scientific research and free thought, quickly transformed Europe into another world. The great problem of life was all at once unmasked. Authority, which then meant the selfish reservation for the few, broke down, and reason, dazed and tottering in the sunlight which burst through the gloom of ignorance, scarce realized the transition. But this knowledge, this truth, so far as we apprehend it, while as such so precious, has nevertheless brought its due proportion of pain. Reason, search as she will, can vouchsafe no satisfactory answer to the universal enigma; problems confront us every day which are by the reason unanswerable. But the intense desire to find solution, the alternations of grief and joy which mark the character of the search, the great unrest, and the serene repose which a true faith has yet over reason—all these qualities are the web and woof of the art of Beethoven. Take his sonatas, those epitomes of life in music—has any poet, any teacher, given us more perfect work, more organic unity, more vivid contrasts of light and shade, more beauteous colouring, more concentred passion, more serene repose? No, they are the most perfect specimens of art, as such, in the world.

The perfection of Greek art lies in its principles

of harmony and repose; the perfection of mediæval Christian art — the Gothic — in the unfolding of its root idea of the correspondence of life with aspiration; the perfection of modern art is to show the complex nature of modern life, to declare to us its unity under seemingly conflicting principles, to assure us of its beauty and its joy, and to bestow upon us the calm not of contemplation of the past, but of the recognition of the wisdom of the present. It is a result, then, that is reached by the consideration of all the forces which enter into modern life. This is the province of Music. She is the mistress of the emotions, and our claim for Beethoven is that he is the poet and the prophet of the modern world, and that in him Germany completed the circle of her tone poets, and gave Europe a heritage of beauty than which no age or nation has bequeathed a greater.

Thus, for the moment, we take leave of music — a tribute to the genius of the past, to those great souls who live in the memories of men, who assuage our griefs and sorrows, bring peace out of discord, and bear death into a more glorious life upon the strains of melody and the pæan of immortal hope.

INDEX.

A.

ACADEMY of music at Rome, foundation of, by Gregory the Great, 45
'Acis and Galatea,' 150
Advent of the Spirit of Love, 37
development of music after Christianity, 41
Æschylus, 31
Agricola, 87
'Agrippina,' 145
Albrechtsberger, 208, 214
Alcæus, 26
'Alceste,' 165
Allegri, Gregorio, 80
Amatis, 91
Ambrose, St., 44
Apollo Musagetes, 25
Apsarasen, 8
Aquinas, St. Thomas, 47
Arion, 26, 31
Aristotle, 33, 34
Aristoxenus, 33
Arkadelt, 61
'Artaserse,' 161
Augustine, St., 44

B.

Bach, Emmanuel, 175
his influence on Haydn, 182
Bach, Johann Christopher, 108
Bach, Johann Michael, 108
Bach, Johann Sebastian, 117
influence of Reinken and Buxtehude on, 107
influence of Luther on, 118, 119
growth of the Bach family, 120-22
character of, 124-25
organist at Arnstadt, 124
influence of Buxtehude on, 126
stay at Mühlhausen, 126
visits Weimar, 127, 128
visits Köthen, 129-32
his work at Leipzic, 132
the Passion music, 134-36
Bach, Veit, 120
Balbulus, Notker, 46
Barbiton, 27
Bardi, Count, 88
Bayaderes, 8
Beethoven, Ludwig, 200
supremacy of his genius, 201-203
childhood and early years, 203, 204
visits Mozart, 204, 205
his friends, 206, 207
goes to Vienna, 207
tuition under Haydn, 207
peculiarities of his character, 209, 210
loss of hearing, 212, 213

218 The Growth and Influence of Music

Beethoven, Ludwig, evolution of his genius, 213-16
    qualities of his art, 215
Bernard, St., of Clairvaux, 46
Biber, 106
Böhme, 120
Busnois, Antoine de, 58
Buxtehude, 107

C.

Caccini, Giulio, 89
Caldara, 92, 153
Canon, 54-60
Canonists, 33
Cantus firmus, 54, 68
Carissimi, Giacomo, 80-83
    rise of oratorio, 80, 153
    Opera and Oratorio compared, 81
Cavaliere, Emilio del, 81, 88, 89
Cecilia, St., 43
'Chandos Anthems,' 150-54
Charlemagne, 45-48
Chelys, 34
China, 3-6
    growth and dissemination of music in, 3-6
    characteristics of the Chinese and Hindus compared, 4
    Chinese scales, 5
    limitations of tonal art in, 5, 6
Choruses (Handel's), 155
Chrysostom and Cyprian, SS., 44
Cithar, 34
Colonna, 153
Comedy, origin of, 30
Conduit, 54
Corelli, 91
    influence over sonata, 179
Corsi, 88
Counterpoint, 54
    double, 55
'Creation,' Haydn's oratorio, 186
'Crux Fidelis,' 78
Cymbalum, 34

D.

Devadasi, 8
'Die Zauberflöte,' 196
Diodorus, 33
Dionysus, worship of, 25
'Don Giovanni,' 196
Drama, Greek, 30
Dufay, 57, 76
Dürer, 119, 120

E.

Early Church music, 43
    efforts of Constantine, 44
    establishment of Church music by Ambrose, 44
    Gregory's innovations, 45
    development of five-lined staves, 46
Egypt, 10
    characteristics of, 10
    qualities of Egyptian art, 11, 12
    systems and associations of Egyptian music, 12, 13
    musical instruments of Egyptians, 13
Ephraim, St., 44-46
Erato, 25
Esterhazy, Prince, 177
'Esther,' Handel's first oratorio, 150
Euclid, 33
Euripides, 31-33
Euterpe, 25

F.

Florence, 84-87
Flute, 13, 34
Franck, 108
Franco of Cologne, 47, 53
Franco of Paris, 55
Frankh, 173
French school (earliest), 52
    influence of Paris upon culture, 52
    influence of Crusades, 52-53
    establishment of musical school in Paris, 53

Index

Frescobaldi, Girolamo, 93
Froberger, 106
Fürnberg, Baron von, 176
Fux, Johann Joseph, 108

G.

Gabrieli, Andrea, 88
Gabrielis, 75
Galilei, Vincenzo, 88
Gallo-Belgic school, 56
    Dufay's genius, 57
Gandharven, 8
Garlande, Jean de, 54
'Giulio Cesare,' 149
Gluck, 159
    incidents of early life, 161
    first operas, 161
    visits London, 162
    Handel's influence, 162
    Rameau's influence, 162
    returns to Vienna, 162
    his opera 'Orfeo,' 163-65
    his opera 'Alceste,' 165
    goes to Paris, 166
    reform of French opera, 167-70
    his work as an artist, 170
    his operas 'Iphigénie en Aulide' and 'Iphigénie en Tauride,' 166-70
Gombert, 61
Gopis, 8
Gothic architecture, 53
Goudimel, 76, 77
Greece, 20
    Palestine and Hellas compared, 20, 21
    mental characteristics of the Greeks, 21
    foundations of Greek art considered, 22, 23
    association of Greek music with mythology, 23-25
    historical period of Greek music, 25
    conception of moral effects of tone, 30

Greece, Greek drama, 30
    Plato's conception of music, 32, 33
    decline in the art, 33
    musical instruments, 34
Gregory the Great, 45
Guarneri, 91
Guidiccioni, Laura, 81
Guido of Arezzo, 47, 53
Guilds (musical) established, 51

H.

Hammerschmidt, Andreas, 108
Handel, 138
    Bach and Handel compared, 138-41
    characteristics of Handel's art, 141-42
    goes to Hamburg, 143
    first operas, 143
    visits Florence and other Italian cities, 144
    compositions while in Italy, 145
    goes to London, 146
    his operatic writings, 147-50
    characteristics of English society in eighteenth century, 150-52
    growth of oratorio, 153-56
    'Saul' and 'Israel in Egypt,' 156
    character of the 'Messiah,' 157
Harmonists, 33
Harp, Egyptian origin of, 13
    used by Hebrews, 16, 18
Haydn, 171
    events in his life, 172-77
    his mission in musical art, 177
    development of sonata, 178-82
    development of symphony, 182-84
    influence of Mozart, 185, 195
    Haydn's influence in quartet, 186
    his oratorios, 186-87

Haydn, his last days, 187
Haydn, Michael, 197
Hindustan, 7
    characteristics of, 7
    association of music with mythology, 8
    cause of non-advancement of music in, 9
Hobrect, 87
Horn, 34
Hucbald, 47
Hymn, German congregational, 69

I.

Influence of Italy upon Germany, 106
Intermezzi, 87
'Iphigénie en Aulide' (opera), 166, 170
'Iphigénie en Tauride,' 167, 170
Isaak, Henry, 69, 87
Isis-Hathor, 12
Israel, 15-19
    characteristics of the race, 15
    Hebrew musical instruments, 16, 17
    Temple service, 17
    Influence of Hebrew history upon music, 19
'Israel in Egypt,' 156

J.

Jacopone, 47

K.

Kapsberger, 82
Keiser, 143
Kerl, 106
Kettledrum, 13
Klopstock, 136
Krishna, 8
Kuhnau, 179

L.

'La Resurrezione,' 145-53
Lassus, Orlandus, 61
Legrenzi, 92
Leibnitz, 136
Leo, 153
Lesban school, 26
Lessing, 136
Loreto, Vittorio, 82
Lotti, 92
Lully, Giovanni Battista, 100
    career of, 100-102
    characteristics of his genius, 100-101
Lute, 13
Luther, influence of, 68-71
    introduction of German congregational hymn by, 69
    translation of liturgy by, 69
    use of Volkslieder in Church service, 69
    his influence over Bach, 119
Lyre, 13, 34
Lyric poems, 26
Lyric poet (derivation of term), 27

M.

'Maneros,' 13
Marchand, Louis, 102
Mazzochi, Domenico, 82
Meistersingers, 51
Merullo, Claudio, 88
'Messiah,' 142, 152
    character of, 157
Minnesingers, 50
Minstrels, 50
Miracle plays, 81
'Missa Papæ Marcelli,' 78
Monodic form, 80
Monody, 89
Monteverde, 89
    founder of modern orchestra, 90
Morality plays, 81
Morzin, Count, 176-77
Motette, 54

Index 221

Mozart, Wolfgang, 188-99
    ascendancy of literature and art in Germany, 189, 190
    birth and early years, 191
    characteristics of his genius, 192-94
    development of sonata and symphony, 194-95
    his operas, 195-96
    'The Requiem,' 197-98
Mozart, Leopold, 191
Mystery plays, 81
Muffat, 106

N.

Neri, Filippo, 81
Netherland school, the, 59-62
    characteristics of, 59, 60
    Okeghem, founder of, 60
    chief masters of, 61
Neume notation, 44
Nicolini, 147
Nicomachus, 33

O.

Odington, Walter, 54
Okeghem, 60
Opera, Italian, 81
    birth of, 86-91
    French, 99-104
    Handel's works in, 147-50
    Mozart's works in, 195, 196
Oratorio, its origin, 80, 81
    growth of, 153-58
Orchestra (modern), founder of, 90
'Orfeo,' 163
Organ, 46
Organum, sacred (Hucbald), 56
Orpheus, 24
Osiris, 12
'Ottone,' 149

P.

Pachelbel, Johann, 108
Palestrina, 76-79
    incidents of his career, 77-79

Palestrina, reformation of Church music, 78
    his style, 79
'Paris and Helen,' 166
Part-singing, 47, 56
Part-writing (canonic), 57
Passion music (Bach), 134, 135
'Pastor Fido,' 149
Peri, Jacope, 89
    his operas 'Daphne' and 'Eurydice,' 89
    invention of dramatic recitative, 89
Pericles, 32
Perotin, 54
Phidias, 32
Piccinni, 167
Pizzicato, 91
Plato, his conception of music, 32-34
Plutarch, 33
Polyhymnia, 25
Polyphony, 76, 77
Porpora, 175
Prætorius, Michael, 108
Precursors of the great tone poets, 105-14
    mental qualities of the Netherlander and German, 105
    Italian influence on Germany, 106
    Buxtehude's influence over Bach, 107
    school of Mid-Germany, 108
    mental characteristics of the eighteenth century, 112
    functions of music, 113, 114
Près, Josquin des, 61, 70, 87
Psalter or long lyre, 34
Purcell, Henry, 147
Pythagoras, 28-33
Pythagorean philosophy, 28

Q.

Quartet, development by Haydn, 186

R.

'Radamisto,' 149
Ragas, 8
Rameau, Jean Philippe, 100
   career of, 102
   characteristics of his art, 104
   influence over Gluck, 162
Rebab, 46
Rebeck, 49
Reinken, 107
Renaissance, the, 65-67
'Rinaldo,' 148
Rinuccini, Ottavio, 88
Rondeau, 54
Rore, Cyprian de, 75
Rossi, Michael Angelo, 82
Rota, 46, 49
Rousseau, 168

S.

Sammartini, Giovanni Battista, 161
'San Giovanni Battista,' 153
Sappho, 26, 27
'Saul,' 156
Scales, Chinese, 5
   Doric, Phrygian, and Lydian, 29
   'Plagal,' 45
Scarlatti, Alessandro, 94-98, 153
   his influence, 95, 96
   development of sonata and symphony, 183
   Domenico, 181
Scheidemann, 107
Scheidt, 107
Schein, 108
Schultz, 107
Schütz, Heinrich, 108
Senfel, Ludwig, 70
Singing-schools established by Sylvester, 44
   established by Charlemagne, 46
Sirens, 25
Socrates, 21, 32
Solmization, 47

Sonata, development of, 178-82
   origin of name, 178
   developed by Corelli and his pupils, 179, 181
   by J. S. Bach, 181
   by Domenico Scarlatti, 181
   by W. F. Bach and E. Bach, 182
   by Alessandro Scarlatti, 183
   Haydn's influence, 185
   by Mozart, 195
Sophocles, 31, 33
Stradella, 95, 153
Stradivari, 91
Strozzi, Pietro, 88
Swelinck, 107
Sylvester, St., 44
Symphoniæ Sacræ, 75
Symphony, its development, 182
   developed by Lully, 183
   origin of, 182
   developed by Mozart, 194
Syrinx, 34

T.

Temple service, 17, 18
Terpander, 26
Terpsichore, 25
'The Requiem' (Mozart), 197, 198
'The Seasons' (Haydn's oratorio), 187
Thespis, 31
Thomas of Celano, 47
Thun, Countess von, 176
Timbrel, 17
Tisias, 28
Tragedy (origin of), 30
'Traité d'harmonie,' 103
Tregon, 34
Tremolo, invention of, 91
Troubadours and Minnesingers, 48-51
   their compositions, 49
   influence of Crusades, 50-52
   transition from minnesong to meistersong, 51
Trumpet, 34

Tympanum, 34
Tyrtæus, 25

U.

Utrecht 'Te Deum' and 'Jubilate,' 150

V.

Vedas, 8
Venice, 73
Violin, 46
Volkslieder, 69

W.

Waldstein, Count, 207
Walther, 71
Willaert, Adrian, 61
    initiates harmonic combinations, 73-75
    establishment of polyphony by, 75
Winckelmann, 136
Wittenberg sacred song-book, 71
Wolf, 136

Z.

Zachau of Halle, 143
Zeelandia, 57

THE END.

www.ingramcontent.com/pod-product-compliance
Lightning Source LLC
Chambersburg PA
CBHW021814230426
43669CB00008B/749